DANEY PARKER

THE PUSH OVER

Contents

For my mother

Prologue

2.00 am Monday, 3 June 1996

It's graveyard shift at the Samaritans office in a small town in Surrey. The two volunteers on duty are usually left undisturbed at this hour, so the phone ringing startles them both.

The call is answered on the second ring: "Hello, Samaritans, can I help you?"

There is silence at the other end of the line. The volunteer tries again.

"My name is Charlotte. Do you want to tell me your name?"

After a few seconds, the caller speaks, barely above a whisper: "Grace ..."

"Hello, Grace, is there something you want to talk about?"

There is the sound of an intake of breath, then: "I murdered ..."

Charlotte stays quiet, straining to hear what Grace says

next, but she can only make out muffled sobs before the line goes dead.

Chapter One

2:05am, Monday 3 June 1999

I slowly put the phone down on the desk and wait for my shaking to subside and my vision to clear. I want to scream, tear out my hair, throw the phone against the wall, bang my head repeatedly on the desktop ... These are all tactics I have tried before, but they never help.

When I can't sleep, which is most nights, I usually get up and watch TV. I can never concentrate on the screen, though, as my mind watches another show, one that I have on repeat in my head. I see the events of that day, my wedding day, unfold again and again. Always with the same end.

When did it all go wrong? Was there one key moment when I stopped being a regular person and stumbled onto the path that ended up with me becoming a killer?

I want to be ordinary again. I get through each day well enough, acting as if everything is fine. I smile, I talk, I work, I eat. It's at night that my conscience likes to torture me. To end the pain, I go through different options in my head. Killing myself used to be option number one, but I have only got as far as swallowing some paracetamol. Never enough, so far.

I am desperate to share this agony. But whom can I tell? A priest? I can't step foot in a church thanks to my mother putting the fear of God into me. The Samaritans? I never get much further than saying my name. A therapist? How can I find the right sort for my particular dilemma? There can't possibly be therapists trained to help murderers regain their peace of mind.

Tonight, I switch on the computer and start typing.

Confession, Part One

The person I killed on my wedding day could easily have been someone else. There are three others, on occasion, I have wished dead. I have succeeded in despatching with every one of them, one way or another.

In chronological order, victim number one is my mother. She made sure I had all the ingredients for a happy childhood; she also made sure that I didn't enjoy it very much. Mummy wanted to save me from my innate badness.

Her first attempt, that I recall, happened when I was around four years old.

The day started so well. There was a picnic in the garden, the only childhood picnic that I can remember having. I see the four of us sitting in our neat garden on a red, green and yellow tartan rug. Jupiter, our King Charles spaniel, kept trying to steal the food off our plates. Daddy took a lot of pride in the garden and our lawn had bowling-green-quality stripes. We had six-foot-high wood-panel fencing separating our green patch from the neighbours', which meant they couldn't look in from their gardens.

I used to love playing out there – I would take my dolls out for constitutionals in their smart, navy-blue pram, while my brother, Mark, would kick a ball and I would worry he would damage Daddy's tomato plants. Mark had no intention of harming Daddy's plants, though. He wanted to harm me. He would aim the ball straight at me, or kick me directly, if no one was watching. Mark is the person I used to imagine killing the most often.

That afternoon, Mark and I were not fighting. We were too busy eating sickly iced fairy cakes and drinking cream soda with Walls Cornish ice cream floating on the top. Mummy was in a good mood, laughing with us. She didn't even tell me off for licking my fingers. But when Daddy started paying me compliments, her smile no longer reached her eyes.

Daddy brought out his camera to take a picture of us all. Mummy didn't approve of photographs, but she sat with us and said "cheese". Daddy said what a great picture we all made. He then said what a pretty girl I was with my long, shiny hair. He said I was like Rapunzel and when I grew up I would have princes queueing outside the front door. My cheeks burned with pleasure. At the same time, I noticed something was happening to one of Mummy's cheeks. It was twitching slightly. I had never noticed it happening before, but I was to see it many times again in the years ahead. That afternoon I didn't know it was a sign. A warning sign.

The next morning I woke up choking, hair filling my mouth. I opened my eyes to see shorn curls covering my pillow. I jumped up. Hair was everywhere. I put my hands to my head to feel short tufts, where before there had been silky, long softness. I screamed and screamed.

Mummy ran into my room. "Sweetheart, whatever is wrong?"

I was too busy crying to get the words out.

"I hope you're not making this silly fuss because I cut your hair? It was getting far too long and difficult. Short hair is so much more sensible in this hot weather."

Later, when my hysteria had subsided and my face was wiped clean of tears, I was able to ask Mummy why she hadn't take me to a hairdresser to get my hair cut, like other people did.

"You don't want to bother with the expense and fuss of all that nonsense," she told me. "It's not good for girls, sitting staring at themselves in a great, big mirror whilst some fool of a woman makes a fuss of her. Look what happened to Marilyn Monroe!"

"Who is Marilyn Monroe?"

"She was a bad woman who spent all her time putting on makeup, doing her hair, and wearing tight clothes. She died young – she was killed by her own stupidity. If she hadn't been so bothered about her hair, she might still be alive today."

Mummy might not have been fussed about her own

hair, but it didn't stop her dying when she was also young. Not as young as Marilyn, but still too young.

You might think Mummy's warnings would put me off being vain. But I have always loved playing with my hair and makeup. I'm a complete sucker for a beauty counter – can't resist spraying on perfumes, smearing samples of foundations and lipsticks on my hand. Even through all the dramas, I have always put on my face. My brave face.

I like to imagine myself as one of those women in hairspray adverts that jaunts out of the house swinging her hair. Most mornings I wash it, dry it, and set it in heated rollers. I don't know why I bother. Skye, my next victim, pointed out I wasn't doing myself any favours.

She once said: "There's nothing worse than when you see someone with beautiful hair, but with a plain face. It is such a let-down. It makes you look uglier than you are, Grace."

Skye wasn't known for her tact. I used to ignore her insults and just take the good part of what she was saying. There was usually a backhand compliment in there somewhere if you looked hard enough. Skye was lucky enough not to need to bother with her hair. She could get away with a short crop as she had such refined features. You could almost hear whole rooms gasp when she walked into them because her looks were so startling.

Skye said she wasn't vain because she never spent any time getting ready. But she lived by her looks. They certainly helped her to land her job in TV as a presenter.

Skye betrayed me and Mummy messed with me, but they didn't deserve what happened to them. They both loved me, even though they bullied me. Mummy used to say: *"I hate wounding you, darling. It kills me to punish you, but heaven would be a sad place for me without you there, too."*

Right until the end, Skye was always telling me how much she needed me; she thought I needed her, too. She had no idea that I was tired of our friendship, but then she couldn't see much beyond her own needs.

If she were here now, she could tell you all about herself at length. She thought every detail about her life was fascinating. Well, perhaps it was. I certainly thought she was brilliant company when I first got to know her.

I met her on my first day of college. A big day for me, a big day for all of us first years. It began at Leeds station, there was a group of about ten of us standing awkwardly with our luggage, waiting for the minivan that would take us to our college on the outskirts of the city.

A girl wearing a man's baggy suit trousers, a pin-striped shirt, and bright, red braces, was closest to me. She turned to look at me and smiled. She had gleaming white teeth, so when I smiled back, I kept my lips together to hide my inferior teeth.

"Hi, I'm Skye. This is weird."

"Hi, Skye, I'm Grace," I said, and once I started speaking, I couldn't stop: "I know exactly what you mean. Most of us don't know anything about what lies ahead of us, really, and yet we're all standing here attempting to exude confidence. We're probably all feeling lost and unsure of ourselves, as we don't know anyone. So you end up desperately talking to everyone you meet, with no idea who is going to end up being your friend, and who you'll want to avoid for the next three years—"

Skye snorted. "Sorry? I meant the weather is weird."

Humiliation must have been written all over my face because Skye laughed and said: "Sorry, Grace, I was teasing you. You're right – it can be a minefield making new friends. So I'll tell you right now, to put you out of your misery: I am going to be your friend. I am going to be the best friend you have ever had."

And she was for a while before she became the worst friend I ever had.

In those first few terms we had a ball. I thought once Skye got to meet some cool people, she'd drop me, but she never did. Our rooms were just a few doors apart in the halls of residence and Skye was always knocking on my door, asking me to come out with her. She always had a plan.

Most nights, Skye wanted to head out to a bar first to have a few pints, to get in the swing of the evening. I would stick to water, as I was a lightweight when it came to drinking. Then we would find somewhere to dance, or see a band if there was one playing. On Fridays we went clubbing, to the Warehouse to dance to Soft Cell, Frankie Goes to Hollywood, and The Smiths. I couldn't afford to buy drinks there, but Skye was happy to accept free drinks from smitten boys. I got offers, too, but I felt it was politically incorrect to expect men to buy me drinks, so I always refused.

I would make my own way back, as Skye was usually going back with someone she'd picked up. The next day I would hear all the graphic details. I lived vicariously through her sexual adventures, as I was, much to my embarrassment, still a virgin. This would come as a huge relief to Mummy, who told me in all her letters that she was praying constantly for my virtue to remain intact.

Chapter Two

CAR PARK IN TOWN CENTRE
MUST CLEAN UP ACT

By Grace O'Neill

An overflowing litter bin, cans, cardboard boxes and other
unsightly pieces of rubbish are just a few of the sights you
will see in Dashford central car park. According to local

Monday, 10 June 1996

I'm woken up by the smell of fear. Then I feel movement
beside me. I open my eyes and scream. There's a bird's
wing, broken, sadly flapping upwards, attached to a dying
pigeon. A present from Miro, who is crouching close by
making deep-throated cat growls. I leap out of bed, and run
out the room and into the bathroom, where I slam the door
behind me.

No one else is going to sort this out, so I calm myself

down by doing long exhales and telling myself I'm not afraid. After five minutes, I open the door, go downstairs, and fetch a carrier bag and rubber gloves. It is always easier to handle such things when you're wearing rubber gloves.

I then have the charming task of finishing the bird off, which I do by placing it in the bag until it suffocates. Another death by Grace. Maybe I should become a professional hit woman, make use of all the skills I have learnt. I hope this will be the only body I have to handle today and that the cats don't devastate any more wildlife. I find out later that, although Miro and Blake are not going to bring any more bodies into the house, there will still be one more dead body for me to deal with today. But it will be at work, not at home.

Miro and Blake don't understand why I haven't given my first thought of the day to feeding them, and as I carry out the body disposal, they mew extra loudly, demanding to be fed. Eventually I do feed them, but without making a fuss of them like I usually do. Not that they care – all they want is the food.

As I'm up early, I have plenty of time to do my hair and cook a boiled egg for breakfast. I put on my work "uniform" which is black trousers and a bright shirt. Always silk – Conrad made me replace all my cheap, dull blouses with jewel-coloured silk ones.

The walk to work takes thirty minutes which means it makes sense to wear flat sandals. Fine by me; I feel too tall in heels. Although it's not raining, I carry a light-beige raincoat, just in case. Before the high street, I pass the Green. I never walk across it because I don't want to risk stepping on dog mess. The newspaper office is above Oxfam and the fishmonger's in the centre of town.

The Dashford Times goes to press Wednesday night, so

Mondays aren't too hectic. Not that any days are mad here. There are plenty of upsides to living in a leafy part of Surrey, but working for the local paper highlights the downside. The stories I start working on today are:

A graffiti clean-up operation at bus stops.

The disappearance of council planters outside the recreation centre.

Parking restrictions extending beyond the centre of town.

That's as exciting as it gets. Since my own modest killing spree, there have been no murders or other notable crimes committed around here. John, my editor, is relaxed about this, and doesn't expect me to astound him with dramatic news items. Not like Conrad, the previous editor. He was always on at us reporters, demanding we try harder. I would do my utmost to earn his praise – at work, that is. At home, it was another matter. He was kindness itself. I would never have asked him to marry me if he'd been a bastard at home as well as at work ...

When I get to the office, I immerse myself in the petty grievances of local residents and write stories. At lunch time, I have a sandwich in front of the computer, whilst catching up on emails and faxes.

Today, I'm interrupted by John bounding over to my desk. "Grace O'Neill! Put that sandwich down! Let's go out somewhere. It's such a nice day. I'm in the mood for something from Franco's."

"I don't think you understand, John, quite how delicious my sandwich is today. I couldn't possibly think of replacing it with one of Franco's offerings."

"I will give you ten minutes to eat that sandwich, but then I demand you come out and have a coffee with me."

"You buying?"

"I will also treat you to a doughnut."

"Okay, I'm in. Although please promise me that you will not mention poorly sited road signs, bad typography, or apostrophes."

John sighs. "That's very hard for me, when there is a sign just outside this office that combines all of those attributes."

I smile, "Try to keep it for our next editorial meeting. It sounds like a shocker, and you don't want to talk too loudly in this office or some other reporter may try to steal the story."

We walk out of the office and down the cement stairway at the back of the building that always smells of dead cigarettes as it is the main smoking area for the office. As I look down the stairwell, I imagine how easy it would be to slip and fall. If you landed on your head, that would be it.

Soon, John and I are sitting opposite each other in Franco's. I'm flushed because I had to almost run to keep up with John's fast pace. John has a ham and salad sandwich on brown bread in front of him, whilst I have a chocolate-iced doughnut. The table is covered with a red gingham checked tablecloth that clashes with John's blue checked shirt. The tablecloth is made out of paper. Franco's isn't posh, even though it does the best coffee in town. There are posters of racing cars on the walls, the cars gleaming in airbrushed glory. The café is clean, functional, and run by Franco, who always greets me with a cheery "Ciao Bella!".

I lean forwards and whisper to John: "You don't think that perhaps Franco isn't his real name? He is so archetypally Italian, it is almost suspicious ..."

"Let's do some checking up on him when we get back to the office," John whispers back. "Just think how great it would be for our careers if we unmasked a local spy. Or perhaps he is hiding his identity because he has a dark secret. Perhaps he is a murderer!"

Suddenly I don't feel like continuing this banter, so I let John move on to one of his favourite subjects: how his quiz team is performing. He tells me the team is on such a winning streak, the other local teams are getting fed up, so he wouldn't be surprised if the team were asked to move to another pub. He also talks about how he should use his general knowledge to get on some sort of quiz show on TV. I'm not fascinated, but not bored either. I would rather listen to John than be left with my own thoughts.

Back in the office, it is time to do my calls to the emergency services. No luck, though – there have been no crimes committed over the weekend, not even a house burglary or a drunk-and-disorderly incident. This must be one of the most boring towns to be a police officer in the whole country. You could never come here to learn any decent policing skills. You could, however, become an expert on how to be a friendly presence in the high street, offering directions and cautioning children about the dangers of crossing the road.

I'm about to give up on finding anything newsworthy when a call comes in from an elderly gentleman complaining about an overflowing litter bin in the main car park. This sounds like a picture story. I take the office camera, as our photographer is nowhere to be seen, and rush out. When I get to the car park, I'm thrilled to see that no one has yet tidied up the offending bin. It is in a right state.

Picture taken and story written, I'm done with work for today.

Or so I think.

When John comes over to my desk, I'm completely unprepared for what he is about to say.

"Grace, I have a sad story for you to cover. There was a fatal bike accident around an hour ago on the railway bridge. The cyclist, a man in his forties, was hit by a number D12. There could be suspicious circumstances – the bus driver reckons the cyclist might have been pushed."

As John continues, his voice has a slight tremor, so I realise that this story has really affected him. "You need to get on the phone, speak to the hospital, the police, and the driver. I know it's grim, but at least you don't have to speak to any grieving widow – seems he didn't have a family as he lived on his own."

There is no way I can write this story, someone possibly pushing an innocent person to their death? Is someone playing a sick joke on me?. "Oh, John, can't you do it, as you have all the info? I'm not sure I am the right person ... I don't think I can cope with all that sadness. I'm bound to burst into tears in the interviews and make a fool of myself and the paper."

"For God's sake, Grace," John snaps, "grow up! You're supposed to be a news reporter. You've been working here for over ten years. You'd think you'd jump at any opportunity to write a possible crime story. I could ask someone more junior than you to write this up – give them a break – but it's time you proved you're more than just a pretty, albeit miserable, face in this office. Do some proper fucking work for a change."

Two words stand out in what John just said: "fucking", because John isn't a natural swearer; and "pretty", as he never usually comments on anyone's appearance.

"Is it okay if I get started on this tomorrow, John? Give me time to work out how I'm going to approach it?"

"As long as it's done before we go to press, that's fine.

And sorry for swearing, Grace, but this is big news for us. First proper story that has come in since I started here."

Relieved I have managed to put off investigating the accident (please, let it be an accident) until tomorrow, I head out the door. It is raining quite heavily now, so I was right to bring my raincoat. On the way home, I pick up some supper and two bars of chocolate, milk for me and dark for Ruth, who is coming over to watch a video later.

Ruth is my oldest friend. Our mothers met each other before we were born – they both used to arrange flowers in the church. Not always harmoniously.

Once, Mummy came home from church when I was about ten and threw her pruning shears clear across the kitchen, hard into a cupboard door, making the crockery rattle. We had a lot of Pyrex, so no risk of it breaking, or she might have been more careful.

She hissed: "That woman is impossible!" I knew she meant Ruth's mother Eileen – she was always saying the Eileen was impossible.

"What has she done this time, Mummy?" I noticed my mother's cheek was twitching, as if I needed any more warning signals that a storm was about to be unleashed.

"When you come to church on Sunday, you will see for yourself exactly what Eileen has done. You will be horrified to find that our precious church has been turned into a tart's boudoir. All purple and red, the blooms, completely inappropriate. And they stink of pure sex – the whole place smells cheap! Eileen has no idea about the language of flowers. She really should stick to her day job."

"But she doesn't have a day job," I said, as I hadn't yet discovered feminism.

"Well, she should go out and find one!" Strong words

from a woman who didn't believe it was right for women to get paid for working once they had found a husband.

Despite our mothers' differences, Ruth and I became close friends. Whenever I could, I would stay for sleepovers at Ruth's much grander and far more peaceful house.

After I have eaten supper, the doorbell makes a feeble noise. I remind myself that I must replace the battery. I could get it wired to the mains, but then it could give someone an electric shock. Can people die from ringing doorbells? I have heard that one person a year dies from getting electrocuted by their radio-clock alarms.

Ruth is standing on the doorstep holding out a bottle of red wine. We don't bother with hugs; we see each other too often for any of that. Ruth marches straight into the lounge and lands heavily on the settee. She never did lose all the baby weight, not that she's grossly overweight or anything. Just a bit fat, but don't tell her I said that. She holds out the bottle.

"Glasses!" she orders.

"Sorry I haven't laid them out for you already, madam," I say, dipping my head obsequiously.

"Oh, stop messing around, Grace, and get the bloody glasses. I can't be bothered with small talk this evening. I'm absolutely shattered. The boys have been driving me mad. I need wine, chocolate, and to watch something that we have seen hundreds of times before so that I don't have to think."

I fetch the glasses and the chocolate, turn the video player on, and settle on the floor in front of the settee. We watch a Bette Davis film, the one with the moon-and-stars line, and hardly exchange another word.

Confession, Part Two

The last person I have done away with is Conrad Conway.

I thought he was an unpleasant piece of work when I started at the newspaper. When he wasn't sneering at my stories, it was because he was laughing at my feature ideas or ripping into me for sloppy journalism.

When he interviewed me for the junior reporter job, he looked over my head all the time, as if he were hoping someone better would turn up. I was amazed a few days later when I got the job offer. After I started, Conrad soon made it clear that if anyone half decent had applied, he wouldn't have been desperate enough to take me on. He himself was rather a prodigy. He had become editor of the paper two years earlier, when he was just twenty-five, the youngest editor the paper had ever had.

At the beginning, before we became an item, Conrad's constant griping used to get to me. I had no confidence in my writing, but couldn't think what else I could do for a living. Conrad's criticisms were spot on. I never tracked down any juicy stories, and I didn't like to quote people when they said stupid things, as that seemed such a mean thing to do. This is not the right attitude for a good news journalist: it is important to have a nose for blood and then be willing to go in for the kill.

Conrad's insults were sometime personal, too. He used to criticise the clothes I wore. I didn't look smart enough. But I didn't see what was wrong with wearing jeans when I was stuck writing at a computer all day. Conrad, on the other hand, looked the epitome of professional. Always in a suit, his shoes were so polished they always looked brand new, and his shirts were ironed so well you could have cut yourself on his sleeve creases. He had a way of carrying himself that made you want to sit up straighter when you were near him. He was unpleasant, aggressive, and terrifying. I fancied the pants off him.

I didn't have to wait too long – just three months after I started – before my fantasies about Conrad were realised. I couldn't believe my luck. We got together, I'm embarrassed to report, at the editorial Christmas party.

As the most junior member of the editorial team, it was my job to organise our Christmas night out. This wasn't difficult, I simply had to ask everyone (and there were a total of six of us then) what pub they wanted to go to and get a tenner from each of them to make up a float. They chose the Black Swan, one of Dashford's oldest pubs, right on the riverside.

Inside, the pub is separated into wooden booths, each one holding six people, which was rather convenient. I found myself squashed against the wall, but I didn't mind because Conrad was the one pressing against me.

After a few drinks, Conrad turned his focus on me. He had dropped his office superior attitude, and was funny, charming and attentive. He asked me all about myself, so I told him stories of the crazy things my mother liked to do. Then I got him to open up about himself. He described his overbearing, competitive father who was a Conservative MP. He'd never shown Conrad any affection, but used to enjoy humiliating him by thrashing him at games, in particular squash, but he wasn't above making a game of Scrabble a way to prove that he was better than Conrad.

I heard about Conrad's mother, who never complained and tolerated Conrad's father's many affairs. The stories that made me want to cry were about Conrad's experiences at boarding school, where he had been sent from the age of six.

Conrad could see my eyes filling up and said: "Hey, don't look so sad, Grace, it's not the worst thing to have an unhappy childhood. It hasn't done me any harm. In fact, it's made me more determined to have a good life from now on. To work hard so that I don't ever need to rely on my parents again. I have learnt to avoid people who are like my father, and surround myself with people who are gentle and kind." And then Conrad reached under the table and took my hand.

That night I went back to Conrad's flat. This was the top floor of a 1930s riverside block, with the best views I had ever seen in Dashford. Being so high up, I was pleased to see that it didn't look like it would be easy to fall out of a window, as they opened at waist height.

We talked until the early hours of the morning before Conrad insisted that I sleep in his bed and he'd sleep in the lounge. We kissed and I pressed myself into him. When he moved back slightly, I worried that he wasn't that into me after all.

"Grace, don't get me carried away. I don't want to take advantage of you when you're drunk and tired."

"I'm tired, but I don't feel a bit drunk."

"I don't want to rush things."

So I had to wait weeks. When Conrad decided the time was right, I was surprised to find he was quite the romantic. From scented candles in the bedroom to rose petals on the bed, it was as if he'd mainlined Mills and Boon.

The next morning, Conrad pointed to the pillowcase I had been resting on and laughed. I had gone to sleep too exhausted to remove my makeup, so there was a colour imprint of my face on the Egyptian white cotton. Eye shadow, mascara, foundation, and lipstick made up an impressionist image of me. "Well, if I never see you again," Conrad said, "at least I have this to remind me of you."

Conrad treated me like a princess in bed, but when we were in the office, it was business as usual. He sighed as he read my articles, shouted when I suggested inane feature ideas, and berated me for being sloppy, slapdash, and sentimental. But he treated me just the same as he did everyone else at the paper, so at least he was fair.

This didn't stop the office gossip. You can't get away with having an affair in a newspaper office and expect to keep it quiet. At the time our editorial assistant was a girl called Emma, fresh from finishing her A levels. She was desperate for me to spill the beans.

She cornered me when I went into the kitchen to wash up my mug.

"So, have you got a thing for bastards then, to end up with Conrad?"

"Emma! That's so rude, I have no intention of telling you anything about my personal life."

"Oh, come on, Grace, I want to learn how to be a top investigative reporter like you. You can't expect me not to ask rude questions. Now tell me, what's Conrad like when he's not here? Does he use moisturiser? Does he cook you meals? Does he buy you presents?"

"If I told you anything about Conrad, he'd be furious. He'd be even harder on me at work than he is already. Just so you know, though, I don't have a thing for bastards. Conrad is a big softy underneath.But if you tell anyone I told you that, I will make your life a misery. I will pour salt in your tea, put chewing gum in your hair and find a way to ensure you never get any of the chocolate biscuits at our editorial meetings."

"Ooh, I'm scared, please don't, Grace!"

"That sarcastic tone doesn't fool me, Emma. I know that you're genuinely terrified, despite that grin on your face. If my threats don't scare you, then just remember I'm sleeping with your boss and I can always get him to fire you."

As Emma moved past me to fill up the kettle, she decided to try to scare me instead: "Grace O'Neill, I have been recording your threats, and if anything happens to me, be sure the tape I have secreted on my person will find its way to the proper authorities."

Emma was smart, which is probably why she is now the editor of a top woman's glossy. Perhaps I should ask her if there's any chance of a job for me there? After all, I'm an expert in beauty products ... It's a bit embarrassing, though, to ask an ex-junior to take you on. Highlights what a failure I am.

My mother thought I was a failure for having to work, rather than having found a rich man to support me. Skye thought I was a failure because I let other people walk all over me, meaning my mother and Conrad (she didn't think to include herself).

Her first run-in with my mother was during our first uni summer break. Skye kept begging to come to stay with me during the holidays, even though I had told her a million times about how dull my life in Dashford was. She was staying with her mother at the time, who lived in a commune in a huge run-down mansion just outside Godalming. This sounded ideal to me, but Skye said it was a nightmare, and that she would have loved to have had a normal childhood like mine. She wanted to see the house I had grown up in.

I knew there were going to be fireworks from the minute Skye sat down to eat. Mummy had prepared one of her cele-brated roasts. I had told Mummy that Skye was vegetarian, but she didn't hold with any of that "silly nonsense". When I brought Skye into the kitchen to meet Mummy, at first it seemed that it was going to be okay.

Mummy rushed up to Skye, engulfed her in a tight hug, and exclaimed: "My darling, darling girl. I hear you have been the most wonderful friend to Grace. You are so welcome here. Please make yourself at home. You must tell me all about yourself."

After Skye sat down at the table in the cramped dining room, things went from great to terrible before the first mouthful. My mother's lips started pursing when she asked Skye if she wanted to say grace and Skye said no because she didn't believe in God. Then Skye committed another sin by refusing to eat any of the perfectly cooked lamb.

"I did tell you that Skye doesn't eat meat, Mummy," I said.

"But look at the size of the poor wee girl. You need a good hearty meal inside of you, Skye."

I knew that Skye was not going to be Mummy's idea of a "nice" girl, but I'd convinced myself that Skye would be able to charm her, stupidly forgetting that Skye's charms worked far better on men. Just as well my brother wasn't there – Skye would have been all over him.

Mummy suggested we sit down after dinner with "nice cup of tea" in front of the TV, but Skye said the night was too young to be wasting it sitting inside.

"Why don't you join us and come into town for a drink, Mrs O'Neill? You never know, you might meet a nice man – there must be some talent in this town," she said with a wink.

"Excuse me a minute, dear, I just need to talk to Grace alone for a second. Would you mind leaving us alone in the kitchen?" was my mother's reply.

When Skye left the room, my mother shut the kitchen door and turned to me. "Get that nasty little whore out of my house!" she shouted, her face purple, her cheek twitching so violently she looked like she had been plugged into the mains.

That left me with the problem of finding a way to ask Skye to leave. I opened the kitchen door to find Skye standing directly outside. She had obviously heard what my mother had said.

"Looks like your mum and I didn't quite hit it off. I'll be off. I'm used to mothers not liking me – even my own doesn't seem to want me around."

I hated it when Skye made out that her own mother didn't love her; somehow, it made me feel guilty and that it was up to me to put it right. I was torn. If I left with Skye, my mother would be furious; on the other hand, if I let Skye leave on her own, I knew she would accuse me of being a disloyal friend. In the end, I decided the wrath of Skye was easier to handle, so I walked Skye to the station. Skye gave me the silent treatment and got on the train without even saying goodbye. The next time she saw me, though, all seemed to be forgiven. Which is a shame. It would have been so much better for both of us if our friendship had died there and then.

Chapter Three

Tuesday, 11 June 1996

I feel sick as I begin putting together the story of the tragic bike accident yesterday. I feel guilty, too, as though it was me who pushed the poor man in front of the bus. First, I call the police and speak to an officer called Richard, whom I vaguely know from school, as he was in the same year as me. He says that the only person who believes the cyclist was pushed was the bus driver, which is why it is important to find other people who might have seen what happened. No one who was on the bus seems to have witnessed the accident. Richard says that in his opinion the cyclist skidded, as it was such heavy rain yesterday evening, and it will have to be recorded as an accident unless other witnesses come forward.

I then have to call the driver, which I know is going to be a tough conversation. When I call the bus depot, the depot manager tells me that the driver is called Jenny May and that she has been granted leave of absence. He refuses to give me Jenny's home phone number, but I manage to track it down using my amazing investigative skills. I find her in the phone book.

Not surprisingly, Jenny is distraught over what happened. Her voice keeps breaking as we talk and she has to stop sometimes to calm herself down. "If only it wasn't raining," she says, "I might have been able to stop in time. That poor, poor man, he was on his way home from work, I imagine; he had no idea he would never see his home again. Oh God, his poor wife and kids – have you spoken to them?"

I explain that the cyclist, Jeffrey Manwell, lived alone and doesn't have any family. I tell Jenny that she mustn't blame herself. I have a handkerchief in the hand that isn't holding the phone and I dab my eyes as I speak. It must have been such an awful experience for Jenny. I hate to add to the pain, but maybe talking about it will help. I ask Jenny what she remembers.

"It happened so quickly that it is all a bit of a blur. I was coming up to the brow of the hill at the top of the bridge. I slowed down as I could see there was a man on a bike in front of me, then I moved over to give him room as I was about to overtake. There was a woman walking on the pavement just ahead.

"Next thing I know, the cyclist is down, right in the middle of the road, and I'm on top of him."

We have a long break in the conversation at this point, both of us needing to compose ourselves.

After a while, I ask: "Do you think that the woman you saw pushed the cyclist?"

"I can't swear that she did. I thought I saw her move towards him just before he fell – there was a movement I thought could have been her arm coming out. But I was focused on the road, so what I saw was with my peripheral vision. Surely no one would deliberately push a cyclist in front of a bus?"

"What did the woman look like – do you remember?"

"I noticed that she wasn't holding an umbrella, as I remember thinking that anyone walking in that rain was going to get drenched without one. She had on a light coat and a clear, plastic rain hood. I think I made out long, dark hair. I also noticed that she was pulling a shopping trolley, fluorescent orange with large, white polka dots. I only saw her from behind, though. After the accident, when I stepped down from the bus, she was gone. I asked other people on the bus if they had seen where she disappeared to, but no one else had noticed her."

I don't want to put Jenny through any more, so I thank her, telling her again she mustn't blame herself for what happened.

My next call is to the office of Jeffrey Manwell. He was a solicitor working for a small practice just a few doors down from the newspaper office. I need to track down a picture of him. I speak to a young man who works in the office. He's in shock at what has happened. He keeps saying how he can't believe it – what a careful man Jeffrey was, how he was always lecturing others on safe cycling and the importance of wearing cycle helmets.

It doesn't take long to write up the story. John is disappointed it isn't more meaty, but he agrees there isn't much to go on, and that the evidence of a crime is pretty flimsy. Perhaps we can revisit it, he suggests, if the woman on the bridge is ever tracked down.

When I get home, I need to take some Valium. I can easily imagine pushing that cyclist over, almost as clearly as if I had done it myself. It doesn't take long to give someone a shove – it is such a quick, impulsive movement. A momentary lapse of self-control. How can someone's life be so fragile that someone like me can end it in less than a second?

There is another reason why I need a Valium this evening. Today is the anniversary of my father's death. An anniversary my mother always honoured by wearing black, lighting candles, and not making any dinner. An anniversary I can never forget, as the day he died was the day my childhood ended. I know I need to move on – I know I should have moved on – but I find myself heading to my bedroom. I get down on my hands and knees and reach under the bed to grab the handle of a brown leather suitcase.

I place the case on the bed and sit next to it cross-legged. The suitcase was my father's and his initials are stamped on the front in cracked, black ink: "CRO, Charles Royston O'Neill". I click open the tarnished brass fastenings to be faced with a mess of photographs. I have never sorted them, and they are mostly a jumble of black-and-white, with a few colour ones standing out like jewels. Photos from my childhood, wedding pictures, images of my parents when they were children with their parents, school group photographs, holiday snaps. Some are as big as ten by eight inches, mounted on stiff card; others are strips of passport photos. Ruth and I went through a phase of going into photobooths as teenagers. There must be at least six strips of us pulling silly faces.

Amongst all the family photos, there isn't one of my brother, Mark; it's almost as though he didn't exist, but he was such a key influence of my childhood – a bad one generally.

The first picture I take from the jumble is one of Conrad. It is one his agent used to send out. It is in colour, a headshot. He looks at me with his steady gaze. How can he look so clever just in a photograph?

Next, I pull out a picture of Mummy. Standing outside our front door, wearing a flower-sprigged cotton summer dress. She isn't smiling.

I pick up a photo of Skye in a cropped T-shirt and tightly belted jeans, holding an ice cream and leaning against a tree, pouting. I remember taking that shot just before our summer exams. We had gone to a park to "revise".

The last picture I remove is the one that I have been looking for. A newspaper cutting headed by a picture of Daddy. It is his death notice.

I wish – how I wish – I could see him again. Tell him about all the years he has missed. I haven't achieved much, but I know he would still be proud of me. I think he would even forgive me for killing someone. He would blame the victim, not his perfect daughter Grace.

His illness seemed like nothing at first. I was just six years old. The morning of the day he went into hospital, he was sitting in the back garden, in one of our deckchairs, his arms widely outstretched as he was reading what I used to call a "clever paper". Jupiter was sleeping at his feet. When I went out into the garden, Daddy leapt out of his chair and chased me around the garden. Jupiter jumped up, too, happy to join in the game. I thought Daddy was the worst runner in the world because no matter how slowly I ran, he could never catch up with me. And then he fell and stopped moving. I thought we were just playing a game, but the game went on and on. Jupiter's barking alerted Mummy, who came out, calmly felt for Daddy's pulse, and told me everything was going to be okay but that I needed to go inside and dial 999.

When Daddy was in hospital, I never thought it was anything serious. I used to look forward to the hospital visits. I would march down the ward in my dress-up nurse's uniform, saying hello to everyone. I liked to chat to the other patients because Daddy was always asleep.

I didn't know he was going to die.

Even when they moved him into a room of his own, I didn't know what that meant. He was only in that room for two days. One evening, I was sitting watching *Nationwide* on the TV in the lounge with the door open, when I heard Mummy say some dreadful words into the telephone in the hallway. She said she had some sad news and that Charles had passed away.

Why had no one told me? I threw myself down onto the lounge floor and started screaming.

My screaming did not go down well with Mummy. She said that it was bad enough that her husband had died, without having a difficult child to deal with, too. Whenever I cried after that, she'd get furious with me, telling me that Daddy would be cross with me for feeling so sad.

Not only was I not allowed to grieve, I was also discouraged from ever talking about Daddy. Mummy never mentioned him; neither did Mark. The only creature who openly showed emotion was Jupiter, who used to sit forlornly at the front door every evening, whimpering when his beloved owner did not come home.

No matter how much I cuddled Jupiter to comfort him, he never again was the bouncy, happy dog he had once been. Less than six months after Daddy died, Jupiter died, too. I think it was partly from a broken heart.

Now, the newspaper clipping in my hand, I sit quiet and still, my mind back to that awful time when my happy childhood ended. My mobile makes a pinging sound next to me on the bed to break the spell. A text from Ruth: *"Do you want some home-made fudge?"*

I should ignore it, but I make the mistake of replying *"No"*.

She texts back: *"OMG I knew you'd be in a state today, but didn't think it would be this serious. I'm coming in!"*

Sure enough, I soon hear the doorbell making its feeble call. When I open the door, Ruth holds out a Tupperware container.

I don't reach out to take it from her. "That's really kind, Ruth, but I really don't want any. I'd invite you in, but look at my hair. It's a state."

Ruth pushes past me. "I don't care if you look crappy; it makes me look better in comparison. As for the fudge, its isn't for you – it's for me. You can watch me eat it all and get some happiness from thinking how much fatter than you I am."

Ruth heads for the lounge and puts the container on the ledge above the gas fire. She then moves to the window and pulls open the velveteen curtains, as I like the house to be in darkness when I feel I'm in a dark place, and Ruth knows this. "Coffee, please!"

Obediently I go to the kitchen. When I return, I notice that Ruth has been tidying up a little. The cushions looks decidedly plumper.

Somehow, I manage to force down enough fudge to feel sick. Ruth's cooking is irresistible. She has shared a few of her tips with me over the years. Number one, always use butter when you can, never any margarine.

Ruth gets fed up with the lack of conversation and asks me to speak to her.

"Sorry, I'm not in the mood for chatting."

"Are you in the mood for listening?" she asks.

"Just about, as long as you don't tell me anything too exciting."

"That's good, as nothing remotely interesting has happened. Although my kettle has broken. Horace thought it might be a good idea to melt chocolate in it, as he thought that is how you make hot chocolate. So it looks like we will have to buy a new kettle."

This is exactly the level of conversation I can handle. Ruth insists that at the weekend we go on a dull outing – a trip into town to replace the kettle.

Two days later, I pick up Ruth, driving my mother's old VW Golf. It is on its last wheels and looks tatty partly because someone has stolen its VW badge. There is rather a fashion for these badges right now. I can't afford a new car, and when this one dies I don't know what I'll do. I can't start cycling everywhere – apart from the danger, I'd get helmet hair.

When we get to the high street, Ruth prays to the parking angel – the only angel we both still believe in. Parking angel comes up trumps with a spot right outside Robert Dyas. Inside, there is a dizzying range of kettles to choose from – different sizes, shapes and colours. I'm just thinking that there may be a *Dashford Times* consumer article to be made out of this, when John appears at the other end of the aisle. This is where it gets very exciting. John, wait for it, is looking for a new frying pan.

Ruth's husband, Graham, is in the same quiz team as John. Dashford is one of those places where you bump into the same people wherever you go, so it's probably inevitable that Ruth would be friends with John. They begin an animated conversation, to which I contribute nothing, on the best kettles and frying pans they have ever owned. After a great deal of analysis, they help each other choose the perfect items. I would have just gone for the cheapest.

Outside, we stand on the pavement whilst John and Ruth continue their kitchenware conversation. I zone out. As I feel the sunshine warming the skin on my bare arms, I remember the weather of my wedding day when it was wet, miserable, and cold. I woke up that day in my old bedroom at home, roused by Mummy coming in to pull up the pink roller blind. "Shame about the weather," she tutted.

She tutted later when I did my makeup; she tutted when the hairdresser arrived; and she tutted when the wedding bouquet of peonies was delivered. It was all such a disappointment to her – not the wedding she'd envisaged for me at all. She wore black that day, not because she was in mourning but because I was getting married in a Register Office. As it turned out, mourning clothes should have been the dress code.

I hear my name being said and I snap back into the real world.

"Grace, what do you think?" asks Ruth.

"It's a great kettle," I reply.

"Oh you haven't been listening again," says Ruth. "I asked if you're free tonight. John is coming over for a takeaway curry. I'm not sure I can stand hearing him and Graham banging on about obscure facts that might come in useful in the quiz."

I hold up my hand and shake my head. "Sorry, I can't come."

"Why ever not?"

"I have scheduled some serious moping. It is June."

Ruth puts both her hands on my shoulders and gives me what she thinks is a little friendly shake. I can feel my teeth rattle. "Oh, come on, Grace, take a night off. You can be miserable for an extra day in July."

So here I am, on a Saturday evening in June, out. Just because I'm out, though, doesn't mean I'm having much fun. The food is good, though. I don't know whether it is because Ruth is an only child, but she doesn't like to share her meals, so I know better than to try any of hers. I help myself to everyone else's dishes, and they dig into my korma.

It is just us four adults sitting around the table. The boys are in bed, clearly not sleeping. The evening is punctuated by thuds that shake the whole cottage and screams that sound serious.

Ruth and Graham take it in turns to rush upstairs, but they are soon back down to say that the boys are fine. Just a fall out of bed. Just the TV falling off a desk. Just a wardrobe door being ripped off. Horrible Horace and Fighty Fergus (as I call them) create a devastating amount of havoc for such little people. This house is always full of noise, mess, and fighting. Even Ruth and Graham's cat, Boris, is a great big bruiser, who hisses when you go near him, and that's when he is not pushing knickknacks off the mantelpiece to smash onto the floor when he wants attention.

After we have eaten, John says he has a brilliant idea. I'm not expecting much, but I'm still disappointed.

"As there are four of us, we should play bridge," he says, rubbing his hands together in joyful anticipation of a positive reaction to his suggestion. He has no idea sometimes.

"Grace can't play," says Ruth.

"We can teach her," says John.

That's when I start laughing.

I thought my life was dull, apart from the murder and constant after-murder, post-traumatic stress I suffer, but now I realise it could get a whole lot duller. My laughter begins to get a bit out of control, and I worry I won't be able to stop, but Ruth helps me calm down with one of her friendly "slaps" on the back, which knocks me out of my chair. The twins get their superhuman strength from her side of the family.

Once I have recovered and am sitting back on the chair, I say to John: "Never, ever, offer to teach me to play bridge again. Life in this place cannot get to the point where it is so bad I want to take up bridge. Not even if I live to see eighty."

"If you live to see eighty," says John, "you would be very grateful to be able to play. Apparently it helps to stave off dementia – you'd be a fool not to learn."

"You'd be a fool if you ever mention bridge to me again," I say in as cross a voice as I can manage, which comes out a bit squeaky.

John snorts. "What exactly would you do to me, Grace?"

If only he knew what I am capable of. I do not tell him of my past record of disposing of people who cross me. Instead, I compose myself and say that I think I'd better leave before someone suggests doing something even more exciting, like filling in a tax return.

John offers to drive me home, as he knows I don't have my car. I don't like other people driving me – I can see hazards all the time that I feel obliged to point out to the driver. Ruth is used to me shouting "red light!", "pedestrian!", "cat crossing!", and knows to ignore me.

The first dangerous move John makes is to start driving before he has put on his seatbelt, so when he does get round to manoeuvring the belt into its slot, he swerves slightly towards the pavement. I grip the sides of my seat and force myself not to scream each time he brakes a fraction later than I would like. To my surprise, we make it safely to my house.

Just before I get out of the car, feeling a bit shaky, I thank John for the lift and apologise for being rubbish company. "I would invite you in for coffee," I say, "but I think I've disappointed you enough for one evening."

John smiles. "Not at all, I've got to get up early for cricket tomorrow, so an early night will do me good. Goodnight, Grace." I peck him on the cheek – rather stubbly but he smells nice, like a garden after rain. John waits until I'm safely indoors before he drives off. At last, I am on my own with still plenty of time to wallow.

Confession, Part Three

The first time I fell in love was during my second year at uni, autumn term. By then, Skye and I shared a house in Headingley with Justin, another student on our media course.

I met Adam at a party. Student parties I went to were not cool. There was never any food and everyone kept their own drinks close by. I had two cans of Tenants Super in a carrier bag by my feet. It was important to guard your booze at these parties. There were no lights on, but there were candles dotted around the room. Seems like a fire hazard waiting to happen now that I think about it, but I was less risk-averse in those days.

Adam came and stood next to me, casually looking around the room, and then he started talking to me. He had shoulder-length hair, large, dark eyes, but was a bit on the short side being the same height as me, and I wasn't even wearing heels. We shouted at each other above the sound of the music, before he asked me to come outside so that he could hear me better.

When we went outside, though, he had no interest in what I wanted to say at all; he leant me against the side of the house and started kissing me.

He walked me home, which was only about a mile away, but it took ages to get back because we kept stopping to do more snogging. I invited him in, and he stayed the night. We didn't have sex – I was too anxious as I hadn't done it before and Adam didn't have any condoms on him.

The deed was done a week later. Boy, what a relief. At the time, I thought the sex was wonderful, but looking back, neither of us really knew what we were doing the first few times and were too shy to give or take instructions. Adam was a virgin, too. We got better at it, though, and after a few months became sex junkies. Skye moaned at me for always being in my room with Adam or for being away at his place.

"For Christ's sake, Grace, can't you go for one day without seeing him? You're becoming one of those sad girls who can't bear to be parted from their boyfriend."

I did worry that I was spending so much time with Adam, but I couldn't help myself. I didn't like to think of myself as a crap friend, so I did try to keep some time free to spend with Skye.

On Wednesday afternoons, we didn't have any lectures, so we'd usually hang out then. One Wednesday, Skye was in her room as she was late finishing an essay (I'd finished it weeks earlier). I was sitting in the front room, which was half kitchen, half sitting room, watching *Countdown*.

Skye walked in, slamming the door after her.

"Fucking essay! I need some coffee. And, Grace, I need to talk to you, too." She went over to the kettle, switched it on, and turned to face me. I wasn't paying her any attention, as I was concentrating on the nine letters on the screen.

"Grace!" Skye shouted. "I said we needed to talk!"

"Training!" I shouted back. "Eight letters!"

"Switch that off, Grace, and listen to me!"

So I did. Skye came over and sat down next to me. She took both my hands in hers.

"I have to tell you about a terrible dream I had last night."

I was irritated that I had been made to switch off *Countdown* to hear about a stupid dream, but I tried to look interested.

"We were on a cruise ship – it was night time and we were standing on deck. Then it got cold, dark, menacing. I couldn't see well. Then I was in the sea, waves higher than skyscrapers. As you know, I can't swim, so I was thrashing around, screaming out to you to save me. I saw you come to the rail of the ship, then Adam appeared next to you. You turned to him and left me to drown. You know I can't swim."

Skye continued gripping my hands, looking at me intently, waiting for my reaction.

I assumed she was making the inane dream up to make

a point. I should have laughed, called her out on it, but I was never brave enough to challenge her.

I gave Skye a hug instead. "I would never, ever leave you to drown. It was just a stupid dream."

"It wasn't just a stupid dream; it was trying to tell me something. I woke up weeping. You don't know how much it hurts me that you don't give a toss about me anymore. You were happy to follow me around like a lost puppy when it suited you, but the minute Adam came along, you dropped me. I expected better of you, Grace."

I didn't want to inflame the argument by saying that I was beginning to have doubts about just how good a friend Skye really was, so instead I told her how sorry I was for being such a disappointment. I promised to change and get our friendship back on track.

I agreed to see Adam no more than three nights a week. I also agreed to treat Skye to a meal out at the local Indian restaurant as a gesture of apology.

Adam was angry when I told him that we had to ration how much we went out together. He said I was being a wimp. We had our first row about it. As it happened, one of our last rows, too, as our relationship was over a few weeks later. I caught him kissing someone else at a party. No prizes for guessing who.

It was one of Skye's favourite past times – stealing other people's men. She said she never meant to do it, but when she was drunk – which was often – she couldn't help herself. Anyway, she would add, she wasn't doing anything wrong; it wasn't her who was betraying anyone. Although, when she kissed Adam, I felt she was betraying me.

I caught them outside the student union bar. A group of us had gone to the bar one Friday lunchtime and had decided to ditch our afternoon lectures. We ended up staying there until late. I don't know how long Skye and Adam had been gone before I noticed they were missing. I went outside to look for them. It didn't take me long to find them, joined together by their mouths, close to the exit. They hadn't even bothered finding somewhere private to go.

I tapped Skye on the shoulder. She disconnected herself from Adam and turned around in drunk slow motion. When she saw it was me, she grabbed hold of my arms, probably partly to stop herself from falling over. Slurring horribly, she said she was so, so, so sorry, that she was a terrible person and I must forgive her as she really, really, really loved me. She lunged towards my face as though she wanted to kiss me. It was grotesque.

Adam, meanwhile, stumbled away from the door and fell down onto his hands and knees. He started throwing up. I was feeling sick, too.

I unpeeled Skye from me and left. I cried myself to sleep that night.

The next morning, I planned to tell Skye that she had to find somewhere else to live. When she came down to make breakfast, I didn't know how to start the conversation, so I gave her the evils instead. You would never guess how wasted she had been the night before – she looked like a vision of loveliness as usual. She really was a complete bitch.

"Hey, Grace, what you looking at me like that for? You in one of your morning moods?"

"Oh, I can't possibly think why I could be cross with you, after what you did last night."

"What did I do last night?" asked Skye, all innocence.

This stumped me for a second, but then I told her exactly what she had done. My voice was calm, but I was shaking. At first, Skye looked flabbergasted, but then she laughed. She said there was no way that what I was saying could be true. Not only would she never do something like that to me, but she thought Adam was a twat. She asked if anyone else had seen her kissing him. Skye concluded that I must be crazy to imagine her and Adam together.

To make it look like I definitely was the crazy one, Adam claimed he remembered nothing about it, too. He came over to see me in the afternoon. He was furious with me for leaving him alone the night before, when he'd clearly been in need of looking after. When I told him why I'd left, he didn't believe me.

That was the end of us. I could no longer trust him, and he couldn't believe what a mad woman I'd turned into. He said I was delusional.

I did consider whether it had been some weird drunken dream, but although I was not completely sober, I was not blind drunk. I know what I saw.

Chapter Four

Tuesday, 18 June 1996

This morning is an early start, as Miro and Blake start playing with my hair at five am and I can't get back to sleep. At eight-thirty, I'm outside looking for another cat. Ruth texted me half an hour earlier: *"Boris not home for breakfast. Worried."*

Boris never misses a meal. I text back: *"On the case. Will check around here before work."*

I'm walking down our road, looking into everyone's

front gardens and calling out, when I see Graham running towards me. He does a lot of running, does Graham, and my road leads down to the park, which is where all the best runners like to show off. Graham must have heard me calling out "Boris! Boris!", because he stops when he gets to me and says: "It's no good trying to get a man by walking down the street calling out for one."

"I would laugh, but I'm too busy looking for your cat. Unlike you."

"I'm running and looking for him at the same time. I know he's just a cat, a great big aggressive one at that, but if he doesn't come home, Ruth will be devastated."

"I do know, Graham, but you have Dashford's number one investigative reporter out looking for him."

"Why, have you asked John to help?"

"Again," I say, "I would laugh at your joke, but I'm focusing on something more important."

Graham runs on. He has a great physique, but I'm only mentioning this as a detached observer. Unlike Skye, I never have designs on friends' husbands, or on anyone else's husband for that matter.

As I approach the Green, I spot something on the side road. A dead animal, definitely. I don't want to go closer; I don't want to look. But I have to. From where I am, I can see orange fur, and Boris is a ginger cat. I steel myself and go towards the poor, dead creature. As I get closer, I realise it is a fox. It must have been hit by a car, and recently too, as the fox looks almost alive, as though it is lying down for a rest. Just a trickle of blood coming from its mouth, and still, glassy eyes.

Sad to see such a beautiful creature killed but pleased it isn't Boris, I'm relieved to get to work, hoping that there will be no more stories of death and tragedy to deal with. I have been dwelling on the death of the cyclist. I call Richard at the police station to find out if any witnesses have come forward, but none have. Richard says the police are not going to pursue it; it is being classed as an accident. But I know too well that accidents are not always as they seem.

With no success at discovering any more about the accident, I turn to the usual work routine of finding out that nothing of note has happened in Dashford. The most dramatic part of the day is when I see that the carpet is beginning to become unstuck near the toilet door, and I point out to John what a hazard this could be. I have already mentioned how slippery the floor is in the ladies, which is a worry, as accidents in bathrooms can be serious. John ignores me. He goes through life blithely unaware of all its dangers. He plays rugby for heaven's sake, so little does he care for his own, and other people's, wellbeing.

Before I go home, I walk to Ruth's house, looking out for Boris as I get near her road. I see she has been putting out "Lost" posters on trees and lamp posts. Ruth does dote on Boris, but I'm no better myself – I am a sad, cat woman.

Miro and Blake were chosen and named by Conrad. Miro is a Birman, quite the most beautiful cat you can imagine – big, blue eyes, the softest, fluffiest fur. Blake is Burmese, not so splendid looking, but much more affectionate. He rushes to the door the second I'm home and follows me around, so it is hard not to love him best.

I would have chosen rescue cats, but Conrad insisted on pedigrees. He had the same breeds when he was a child. He gave me a sob story about how he had fallen in love with these cats, but soon after they arrived he was shipped off to school. He said his mother transferred all her love from him to the cats. Not that he minded, he claimed, as she was so lonely and they were special cats.

When we got the kittens, just a few months before our wedding, it was me, not Conrad, who slaved after them. I fed them, cleared out their litter trays, brushed them, removed their fleas, got up in the middle of the night to give them a sneaky, extra meal. As we were living in his flat at the time, they weren't allowed out, and I felt I had to make it up to them for being deprived of the great outdoors.

Conrad didn't have time to cater to his kittens' every whims. He was working long hours by then, as he was working in the city. It was Skye who first told me there was a vacancy in the newsroom of the cable channel she worked for. She'd wanted me to apply, not Conrad. I didn't have the drive to go for it, though, so I'd encouraged Conrad instead.

With his intelligence, charisma and clear speaking voice, it wasn't long before Conrad was made political correspondent. He was so happy to be working on proper news – London news.

When Ruth opens the door to me, her first words are: "Boris must be dead."

I think she is overreacting, he hasn't been gone for twenty-four hours yet. I give her a cuddle and say I'm sure it will be okay. He's probably locked in a garden shed or something.

Two days later, Boris still hasn't turned up. I also think he must be dead.

I'm sitting with Ruth at her kitchen table whilst Horrible and Fighty are playing war games in the lounge. Ruth has opened some wine, and after a few glasses she turns all serious on me.

"You have to move on, Grace."

"What do you mean?"

"You know exactly what I mean. We all know you have

been through a trauma, but there has to come a point when you try and put it behind you."

"I'm sorry, Ruth," I say and sigh. "I know it must be awful for you, putting up with my miserable presence all the time. I'm doing the best I can. It takes all my energy to get through each day."

"Why aren't you finding it any easier as time goes by?"

"I can't stop thinking about that day."

"Then tell me about the wedding. Tell me about the whole day. Let's go through all your memories from the minute you woke up to the grisly end."

"We don't need to – you were there."

"I want to know how you're remembering it. Talk me through it."

"I can't."

"You can. I know you have it going through your head all the time, so put a voice to your thoughts. For me."

"I will one day. But not now."

"Do it now. Tell me about waking up on the morning of your big day."

I sigh. I would love to tell Ruth everything, confess. It wouldn't be fair, though. But I could tell her about the moments leading up to the murder. So I begin.

"Okay, here goes. As I thought it would be wrong to sleep with Conrad the night before the wedding, I was staying at Mummy's, in my old bedroom. I imagined she would be all thrilled about me getting married at last, but when she woke me, I could tell she was in one of her moods. Something was bothering her, I would find out what that was later. When I came downstairs, she had made the two of us scrambled eggs and smoked salmon, but she sat opposite me with a face full of thunder, so I didn't dare speak to her."

The telephone rings across the other side of the room and Ruth says: "Sorry, I had better get that, it may be about Boris", and rushes to answer it.

She answers the phone, turns around to me, and soon there is a huge smile on her face. She says into the phone: "Yes, he does have white paws! Oh, thank you! Thank you! I can't tell you how happy you have made me."

So Boris must be alive after all. The party is now well and truly over for birds and small animals who live nearby.

After she has ended the call, Ruth whoops and gives me a high five. Well, she tries, but I wasn't quite quick enough to get my hand up in time, so she ends up whacking me on the shoulder.

"A wonderful woman has found my Boris. I'm sorry, Grace, but I have to go. Our conversation will be continued soon, though. No wriggling out of it."

"I'm so happy you're going to get your Boris back," I say, nursing my shoulder as I gather up my stuff to go home. "And I won't avoid telling you everything, though I feel bad about burdening you, yet again."

"I'm used to you being a burden," Ruth says with a grin. "Don't worry about it."

She opens the front door for me and ushers me out.

Confession, Part Four

Conrad and Skye never hit it off. I introduced them at a party in a Soho hotel following a film premiere in Leicester Square. Skye wangled us invites, as she had been asked to do interviews with the stars of the film, interviews which were broadcast live just before the film started. It was a coming-of-age film, so the main actors were teenagers and the party was filled with young, cool, skinny things that made me feel big and old.

Skye was distracted at the party – she had lots of schmoozing to do. She was in her element, flirting, drinking, and I think she must have been snorting coke, too, as she was particularly hyper. I managed to track her down five minutes after we arrived. We kissed on the cheeks, and I proudly introduced Conrad.

"This is Conrad, who you've heard so much about," I said.

Skye glanced at him. "Have I?" she asked.

"What do you mean, Skye, I have been boring you with stories about Conrad for months now ..."

"It's nice to meet you, Conrad," Skye said coldly, then turned around and walked off. She didn't say another word to us.

Conrad was not impressed. "You say Skye is a good friend of yours, but she barely acknowledged you. She was plain rude to me."

"Oh, that's just because she is preoccupied. Skye loves me," I said, despite being rather surprised myself.

"Seems like a funny kind of love," Conrad said, "and she is off her head, which isn't very professional."

"She needs to let off steam when she's been working. Wait until you get to know her – she can be incredibly entertaining."

"I don't think I will ever like that woman," replied Conrad. "She's not my type."

Conrad's friends were not my type, either. A lot of them were from his university days at Exeter. He mixed with a snotty crowd. For example, there was Charlie, who spoke without ever saying a consonant. When I made fun of his accent after I met him, Conrad didn't like it, saying it wasn't Charlie's fault that he spoke that way.

Charlie lived in a house off the Kings Road, Chelsea, the Sloane Square end of Kings Road. The house was painted white in the middle of a terrace of other perfect white houses guarded by gleaming black railings. It wasn't his house; it belonged to someone called Jeremy, whose speaking voice was also grating. There were four of them sharing the place: two boys – I call them boys because they were not mature enough to be called men – and two women, also in their early twenties. They all worked at the same investment bank, earning exorbitant salaries.

Charlie and Jeremy were single at the time. Although the women they shared the house with were gorgeous, apparently they weren't girlfriend material. Most women did not have the right qualifications to be girlfriends, as Charlie and Jeremy had a complex system for rating women that I obviously scored poorly in. It was clear that they did not understand why Conrad had chosen me, as I had the wrong background, the wrong clothes, and the wrong accent.

I often asked Conrad why he was with me when I was so different from all his friends. "Because I love you", was his constant reply. I should never have let him get away with such a glib answer, but it was what I wanted to hear.

Although Charlie must have been mystified as to why Conrad was with me, he was always perfectly polite, although I did catch him looking at me with thinly disguised horror a few times, when I said something dreadful, like when I admitted I wasn't a royalist.

There was a particularly hideous evening at Charlie and Jeremy's house when one of the women living with them decided to throw a dinner party. Not only that, but she cooked all the food herself. I think it might have been part of her plan to ensnare Charlie, by showing him what a good wife she would make one day. I forget her name – it was something like Samantha. She was the nicest person in the house, so I feel bad about forgetting her name, although I will never forget her dreadful cooking. Bless her, though, she tried. She'd attempted to make her own pasta, and thick ropes of dough hung on the draining rack over the sink. It was not appealing uncooked and it was no more appealing when it was. The gloopy pasta dish was followed by a pudding of Angel Delight, the pink instant-whipped blancmange, which was presented in crystal bowls – as if that could make it taste better.

"Don't you love old-fashioned food? It takes me right back to my school days," she said. And everyone, apart from me, agreed wholeheartedly. It must have been a boarding-school thing.

There were sixteen of us sitting around the mahogany dining table. The clinking of champagne flutes and the clatter of silver cutlery on delicate china could not drown out the braying of their voices. Every conversation was a form of one-upmanship. Each person would list their upper-class credentials as if this were a fascinating topic of conver-sation. Mentions of finishing schools, parents struggling to keep the stately home going, all the seasons spent hunting, debutante balls ...

I never joined in, but I would have to field the very occasional question:

"Where are you going skiing this year?" (I wasn't going skiing.)

"Do you have to work?" (I did.)

"Do you keep horses?" (I did not.)

As well as failing the posh test, I didn't share their

general consensus of beliefs. I was not in awe of Margaret Thatcher, and I liked to watch the BBC.

Conrad accused me of being a snob afterwards.

"You hardly said a thing all night," he complained as he drove us home. He had a convertible Saab and as it was a hot summer's evening the roof was down. I had tightly bound my hair in a scarf, but it was still flapping around, and strands kept getting in my mouth, so I replied through gritted teeth: "How can you say I'm a snob? I was the only person there who does my own cleaning."

By then, I had bought a one-bedroomed flat, the top floor of a Victorian house near Dashford train station. Though most of the time I stayed at Conrad's.

"You could do with getting a cleaner actually, Grace, but that's another subject. Just because my friends are rich does not make them inhuman. They have been brought up differently from you. The sour expression on your face every time you're with them does you no favours. You make it clear you think you're better than them."

"Sorry? How can you say that when they think they are so much above me they can hardly see me. I don't feel superior; I feel invisible. They don't like me, so why should I like them? Why you like them is a mystery to me."

"I like them because I made the effort to get to know them. I don't judge them on their facades."

"They have something beneath those awful facades?"

Conrad gripped the steering wheel more tightly. "You're not giving them a chance."

I patted Conrad on the knee, "I know they are your friends, but I have tried. I can't get on with them. Just like you can't get on with Skye."

"Skye!" Conrad spat out. "And you accuse my friends of being shallow!"

Eventually, we agreed to keep some of our friends to ourselves and not inflict them on each other. Conrad would hang out with the Hoorays on the nights I went out with Skye. Plus, he would go on annual golf and ski trips with them, whilst I was happy to stay at home, doing all the things I was embarrassed to do when Conrad was around. Such as eating whole packets of biscuits and watching soap operas on TV. Sometimes, I would go out clubbing with Skye, although I felt so rough the next morning I usually regretted it.

Chapter Five

BUS STOP TRAPS PENSIONER IN OWN HOME

By Grace O'Neill

Local man Mr John Greedie couldn't get his car off his drive last Wednesday morning because of a temporary

Tuesday, 25 June 1996

Today is my anniversary. Two years ago today, I became a wife and a killer. Usually wives don't consider murder until a few years in. I booked the day off work, as I don't plan to get out of bed. I don't want to see anyone, speak to anyone or move. Miro and Blake don't give a toss about my plans and act like it is just the same as any other day. At six am, they start walking on me, licking my face and tapping me with their paws. I feed them and come back to bed.

At eleven o'clock I'm still in bed, looking at the ceiling. I think perhaps I will get up after all, and go to the cemetery. The doorbell rings, feebly; I still haven't replaced the battery. I don't get up. My mobile pings to say I have a message. I ignore it. Then it rings. I switch it off. The doorbell goes again. There is hammering at the door. I get up, go to the door, and shout: "Go away!" I know it must be Ruth outside.

"Grace, open up now! I have had an accident and am bleeding profusely!"

"Go away, Ruth, I'm not falling for that one."

"You have to open up because I really have had an accident – my period has just started and I'm wearing white trousers. Please, Grace!"

I open the door and Ruth pushes her way in. She is wearing dark jeans.

"Ha! Got you!"

As I shut the door, defeated, Ruth barks orders: "Go upstairs, and get dressed in clothes you don't mind getting wet and dirty. We're going on an adventure."

"No, I can't. I appreciate you're doing your best to help me, but I can't. Not that I ever could go on an adventure, even on a good day. You know very well that a trip to the shops is enough excitement for me."

Ruth has her bossy face on, and if I didn't know her as well as I do, I would be scared. Actually, I'm scared because I do know her so well. She says: "Move your arse; get up those stairs now! You have twenty minutes to get ready. I can watch the TV whilst I wait, maybe even have a cup of coffee. You want one? I'll make you one anyway – you'll need the caffeine."

Just over twenty minutes later, I'm sitting next to Ruth

on the settee, drinking my coffee. "Can't we just sit here and watch a film?" I ask.

"No. Trust me, you'll feel better for getting out."

So out we go, and soon we're driving on the A316 over Twickenham Bridge and I have a horrible feeling I know where Ruth is taking me. To the scene of the crime – Richmond.

"Are we going where I think we are?"

"It's time you faced a few demons. We're going to Richmond, but don't worry – I'm not taking you to the Register Office. I'm taking you to the river."

"That's even worse!"

"It's just a river, Grace. Well not any river, the Thames, the best river. You can't avoid it for the rest of your life. We're going to hire a rowing boat."

"Oh, what a lovely idea!" I say. "We can see if we can find any bodies floating past. Or you could fall overboard to recreate my wedding party!"

"Listen," Ruth snaps. "Do you think it's easy being your friend? It is a bloody nightmare spending time with you. You look like the Grace I used to know but act like a zombie. No matter what I try, I can never engage with you; you're always depressed and nearly every conversation ends up with you tearful. But lucky for you, I never give up trying to get you back. Please humour me this once. It's the least you can do."

Ruth has a point: I owe her big time.

When we're in the boat, my knuckles are white as I grip its sides. I didn't want to make a scene in front of the man who hired us the boat, so I managed to hold it together until he nudged us into the water. Now I'm sitting here immobile, useless and terrified. The boat is rocking in a way I hate and I'm far too close to the water. I have not been in a boat for two years; I have not even taken a ferry crossing. I think I'm going to throw up, but I can't even move my head or lean over the side, so I sit still, hoping I don't start heaving.

Ruth pulls hard at the oars. "I don't mind doing this for a bit, Grace," she puffs, "but you can't expect me to do all the hard work."

I continue acting like a statue – I don't speak or move.

After a while, Ruth pulls up to the river bank where there are some steps. "It's your turn now."

I shake my head.

"You don't have a choice. We're swapping places and you're going to row."

It takes a good while of cajoling, shouting, reasoning, and some light physical violence (Ruth shakes me which makes the boat rock in a terrifying manner) until eventually I'm sitting on the rowing bench. Ruth is sitting opposite me on the seat at the end of the boat. "Go!" she orders, so I do.

It is hard work, and soon I'm dripping in sweat. The exertion helps to take my mind off the terror, so I begin to take in the scenery, noticing where I am. I can see Richmond Bridge, with its pale stone and Victorian iron lamp posts, moving further away as I pull at the oars. I can see the tree-lined tow paths and a few people walking along. It is quite a view, almost enough to make you want to take up painting watercolours. The river looks dark grey, reflecting the cloudy sky. There aren't many boats around and my wedding cruiser doesn't sail past us, thank goodness. It is quiet, apart from the slap of the oars as they hit the water and the creaking of the boat.

I have to concentrate to get the oars to hit the water simultaneously, and my shoulders and arms ache from the effort. I don't let myself think about the last time I was here;

I just keep rowing, focusing on the rhythm of the movement. I stop feeling scared; I start feeling exhausted.

"I think we should turn back now," says Ruth. "But as you seem to be a bit of a natural at this, I'll let you carry on."

I don't argue. Although I'm tired, I don't want to swap places again. I don't want to rock the boat.

When we step back on dry land, I feel jubilant. I feel as though I have just climbed a huge mountain. I give Ruth a big hug. "Thank you so much, Ruth."

She pushes me away. "Urgh, you're all sweaty. It's nice to see you looking a bit more alive, though."

When we're back in the car, we devour chicken sandwiches and flapjacks that Ruth has made. Before she turns the key in the ignition to drive away, Ruth turns to me. "Pink cheeks suit you," she says. "You look more human."

"You have succeeded in putting some life back into me," I reply.

But it is not long before I'm travelling back to the usual planet of death, loneliness, and regret. The euphoria begins to fade as I think about what I have just done and where I have been. I get flashbacks of the last time I was on the river in Richmond. I'm not sure if this trip has helped me to set my ghosts to rest or resurrect them. I ask Ruth if she can stop at a florist so I can pick up some lilies to take to the cemetery later.

When I get back into the car with the flowers, Ruth starts on the second part of today's therapy. Getting me to talk.

"Okay, it's time for the next instalment of Grace O'Neill's wedding day."

"You don't have to do all this for me, you know. Take me out, be my therapist …"

"I'm afraid I do. Don't forget that you did the same for me when I fell apart, after Tim."

Tim was Ruth's first love. They'd been inseparable for two years before he finished with her just after A levels were over. Instead of celebrating leaving Woodland Comprehensive, we spent the summer after exams sitting on Ruth's bed, listening to her eclectic music collection on her stereo player. She used to stack her albums on the turntable, from Simon and Garfunkel to Elvis Costello, and they would crash down on one another one by one. I still know the words from "Bridge Over Troubled Water" off by heart. Ruth would shut the windows, draw the curtains, and place silk scarves over the bedside lamp when it got dark. The room would become gloomy and stifling, thick with heat and teenage angst.

Ruth would cry about Tim, moan about Tim, shout about Tim. Excavate every moment of the relationship to pinpoint where it all went wrong. At the end of the summer, Ruth was beginning to talk about how she was going to get over the bastard, and she started playing – and even worse, singing along to – "I Will Survive". She followed a traditional route when it came to getting over a broken heart. I just sat with her. I didn't mind – I had nothing better to do.

I shake my head remembering those "happier" days. "I spent a few weeks with you and then you were better," I say. "I have been broken for years."

"So let's start putting you together again. Tell me about your wedding."

"Haven't you heard enough? What's the point?"

Whining gets you nowhere with Ruth; she tells me I have no choice. In the end, I agree to carry on talking about my Big Disastrous Day.

"Where was I in my tale of woe?"

"You said your mother was in one of her moods. So just a normal day so far."

"Yes, I suppose you're right. I went upstairs and fitted myself into the wedding dress, doing up all the buttons took ages, but I didn't want to ask Mummy to help. When I went downstairs to show off the dress, Mummy looked me up and down. Despite her sour expression, she said: 'You look fit for a prince. Daddy would have been proud.'

"This was just about the nicest thing she had ever said to me. I was hoping that was a good sign, that she was not going to have one of her turns—"

Ruth interrupts, "Shame that turned out to be a false hope."

The car has stopped and we're parked outside the entrance to the cemetery.

"Do you want me to come with you? Or wait here?" Ruth asks.

"I think you've done enough for one day. More than enough. I'll walk home."

I get out of the car and turn into the entrance before I hear the car drive away. Clutching the flowers, I walk inside. It is going to be a long afternoon, and an even longer night.

Confession, Part Five

"An eye for an eye, a tooth for a tooth," Mummy said, but her punishments never fitted the crimes as far as I could tell. Take that time I sneaked a custard cream from the biscuit tin. How was I to know that Mummy used to count all the biscuits to work out exactly how long they would last if we all took our allocated two biscuits a day? I suppose it might have been a bit galling to have her calculations put out, but surely she didn't have to burn Emily?

I didn't know why she was building the bonfire in the garden one Saturday afternoon. I didn't know it was going to be a funeral pyre. It was a cold, autumn day, and I was watching her from my bedroom window as she raked up leaves. Then she came into the house, up the stairs, and into my room. Emily was lying on top of my bed, as always. She had blue glass eyes with dark lashes. She was wearing her best dress made out of white lace that had come from Belgium. Mummy gently lifted her up and told me to follow her.

"Where are you taking Emily?" I asked.

I was not too worried at first, as Mummy seemed calm. Her cheek was free from its warning twitch. In a quiet, low voice, Mummy explained that I was about to find out what happened when people stole. She said that she knew I had taken the custard cream. Now it was time to say goodbye to Emily. She asked me to come out into the garden, where she placed the doll on top of the pile of sticks and leaves before she set fire to the bonfire. Mummy said I had to watch Emily burn. I was too shocked to cry, and anyway, I didn't want to give Mummy the satisfaction of seeing how upset I was.

I rescued the remains of Emily from the ashes of the bonfire the next day and wept as I buried her in a private ceremony. I was very, very angry. Which is why I then did a very, very bad thing.

Whilst Mummy was watching *Songs of Praise* that evening, I crept into her bedroom, opened her jewellery box, and took out a string of pearls, a gold chain, and some silver bracelets from the bottom, velvet-lined section.

Monday afternoon, after school, I took the jewellery out

into the garden shed. I placed it on the work counter, where Daddy had liked to do his carpentry and where his tool box still stood. I took out a hammer and brought it down hard on the jewellery, again and again. The bracelets became misshapen, but the gold chain and the pearls were remarkably resilient. I got the garden shears and sliced into them. Small sections of the chain fell onto the worktop, whilst the pearls went everywhere, scattering, bouncing, and rolling in all directions.

There was a grim satisfaction in venting my anger with all this destruction, but when I was finished, I grew scared. I knew I had to hide my crime. I gathered up all the pieces of jewellery and as many pearls as I could find. I took off one of my school, knee-length socks and stuffed everything into it. Then I shoved the sock behind the back leg of the work bench. I was sure Mummy would never find it there.

Mummy noticed my missing sock before she noticed her missing jewellery. The next day she demanded to know why there was an odd number of white socks in the washing basket. I must have had guilt written all over me when I said that I had no idea. Mummy was cross but not furious; socks did go missing from time to time, after all, and Mummy used to say that the washing machine must have a taste for them.

She didn't notice the missing jewellery until Sunday, when she was getting ready to go to church. I heard the scream, which I had been waiting for, and felt terror.

"We have been robbed!" she cried as she ran out of her room. "Check the house to see if anything else has been taken."

Hours were spent searching the house, but nothing else was found to be missing. Mummy came and stood in front of me, her hands on her hips, a deep frown on her forehead. "Grace, do you know what happened to my jewellery?"

That is the first time I fainted, but not the last – any major stress and I'm out like a light. When I came back to consciousness, Mummy was all kindness and sympathy: "Ah, you wee poor thing, getting so upset over a few pieces of jewellery. Don't you worry about it; it is a sin anyway to get attached to such fripperies. Probably do me good to live a more simple life."

I was amazed that Mummy took the loss so well, and she never did find the sock I had hidden. She didn't, but Mark did.

A few weeks later, he came into my room, holding the heavy sock.

"Greasy," he said, his pet name for me, "I won't ever tell, but you really need to find a better place to hide this." And he threw the sock onto my bed.

He then laughed and added: "I would never have thought you had it in you to be so bad. You're not as boring as I thought. But you're crazy. Crazy, Greasy!" He started stumbling around the room, pretending to froth at the mouth as if he had gone mad. "You're my loopy, deluded, crazy sister, with cotton wool for brains. What have I done to live in this house of mad, mad, mad females?" Then he disappeared before I could talk back.

He was the insane one not me.

I stuffed the sock in the bottom of my school satchel, and threw it into a public litter bin the next day outside of my school. That was the first crime I remember getting away with. Maybe if I had been caught, I would have learnt that it is easier to deal with a fit punishment than to live forever with unbearable guilt.

Chapter Six

FOX STEALS YOUNG CHILD'S PICNIC LUNCH

By Grace O'Neill

A mother was horrified when a fox stole her five-year-old daughter's ham sandwich off her plate whilst they

Monday, 1 July 1996

I wake up after having slept a full six hours, no interruptions. Result. I admit that before I went to bed I did call the Samaritans again. It is pointless, I know, calling and never speaking; I must give it up.

I'm making an effort to think more positively, act more decisively. This morning, I go for a run with Ruth. Our recent outing has inspired us to get fit. Today, we manage to run for a full five minutes before we have to lean against a fence and gasp a lot. We're a bit out of shape. Not like the days when we were queens of the sports field at school. There wasn't much competition, mind – most of the other girls were on about forty fags a day by the time they were sixteen, whereas Ruth and I failed at smoking. We gave up the day we started.

We clubbed together to buy a packet of rainbow-coloured cocktail cigarettes with gold tips when we were fifteen and ended up giving most of them away. We smoked about half a cigarette each before we realised they were not for us; they were disgusting. We weren't much better at drinking either – two cans of anything and we'd be sick. Not like today. Now we can put away a bottle of wine, no problem.

After a minute of rest, Ruth and I run a bit more and then stop for another gasp. We're out for at least half an hour and cover over two miles. Not a bad start.

We're now planning to run a marathon. Not for a while, not for a long while, but one day.

After all this activity, I end up getting to work ten minutes late. John is a bit cross. I don't know what is getting into him lately; he is often in a bad mood.

"You don't take this job seriously anymore," he grumbles as I walk past his desk.

"What do you mean John?" I reply. "I never took it seriously."

"Perhaps you should start trying."

See, he's no fun anymore.

Not long after, John comes into the kitchen whilst I'm making coffee and tells me there is a new staff member I need to meet. A new junior sub-editor. "I thought we could take her out to lunch – that is, if you haven't brought in one of your amazing sandwiches?"

"I didn't have time to make a packed lunch. I went for a run!" I wait for some applause, but I have to be satisfied with a mildly surprised look, one eyebrow raised, not two.

"Good for you. Glad you have some energy for something useful."

At eleven o'clock, the new sub, Charlotte, is introduced to us all as John takes her on an office tour.

I get up to shake hands and notice that Charlotte is even taller than I am. When I look down, I see she is wearing smart, shiny high heels. How can she: a) afford such expensive-looking shoes; and b) walk in them? Damn her.

At lunch time, the whole editorial team (there are eight of us now) go to the Golden Pineapple, our nearest pub. Just as well for poor Charlotte, as it would be mean to make her walk too far in those fancy shoes. Charlotte orders half a pint of lager and sits next to me. She is easy to talk to and has a loud, dirty laugh. I begin to warm to her.

As we're leaving, John takes me by the elbow and asks if I have a minute. So we step back inside the pub whilst the others go ahead. He asks me if I want another drink, but one Coca-Cola is more than enough for me. I let him get me a glass of water, though, as he seems in need of another drink himself. He orders himself a small whisky. I wonder what's eating him?

When he comes back to the table, he looks anxious and I notice his hands trembling slightly as he places the glasses down and then perches on a stool. The stool seems a bit wobbly. I hope he doesn't fall off, although at least he would land on the carpet, so it would just be embarrassing, not deadly.

"I hope you haven't got some bad news," I say.

"Sorry for the big build up," says John. "It's really nothing ... I've got nothing to say, really."

"Then why do you look so worried?"

John makes a funny, gargling sound, which I realise is supposed to be a chuckle. "I don't look worried, don't be silly." Then he reaches across the table and takes my hand. What on earth is going on? I take my hand away.

"Sorry, Grace, didn't mean to step over the line."

"You don't want to get too close to me, John. Look what happened to the last editor who did that!"

"Do you think you could ever imagine going out with your boss again?"

"Why? Are you asking me out?" I say.

I almost spit out my ice cube when he says "Yes".

Oh no. I haven't got time to think of the right way to let him down, so I give a terrible impromptu speech about how right now I can't imagine dating anyone again, blah, blah. Because I'm so embarrassed, I ramble for far too long. Instead of making an uncomfortable situation better, I make it worse. I suggest to John that he tries the *Guardian* Lonely Hearts column if he wants to meet someone, but John says he isn't desperate.

"You must be desperate if you asked me out."

This makes John angry. I seem to have a knack for annoying him today.

"You know what, Grace, I'm getting sick of your self-deprecating comments all the time, and the way you make out your life is so sad. If you think you're so awful and everything you do is so pointless, then do something about it. We all know you have been through rough times – really rough times – but isn't it about time you got over yourself?"

"One minute you want to go out with me, the next minute you tell me how sick of me you are."

We finish our drinks quickly and walk back to work in uncompanionable silence.

This evening is another "Tell Ruth about the wedding" slot. Ruth comes over to mine after dinner and I supply the usual chocolate and coffee.

I carry on from where I left off.

I describe how I was sitting in the lounge on my own waiting for the wedding car to come and collect me, when Mark appeared in the room.

"Oh, Grace," says Ruth. "I didn't know you saw Mark in your house before the wedding?"

"Well I did, he was always offering me brotherly advice before I got married, and I really wish I had listened to him."

Ruth sighs. She never likes me mentioning Mark any more. "Okay, what did he say?"

"He told me not to marry Conrad."

Ruth says: "Shame that you did."

I continue on with the story, detailing how Mummy made a fuss about the fancy car I had arranged to take us to the register office: *"It is only a five-minute walk, such a stupid extravagance. It's not like it is a proper wedding."*

I look over at Ruth. "You know what happens after I arrive at the register office. Why don't you give me a break and describe what happens next?"

"It's your version I want to hear."

"Yes, but the actually getting married bit was uneventful – you could quickly sum it up and I'll correct anything I remember differently."

Ruth sighs. "Okay then, here goes. I was waiting outside the register office in the front garden when you and your mum drew up in that swanky car. Everyone else had gone inside, including Conrad, as you were the last to arrive. I gave you a hug and that lucky horseshoe suspended on a purple satin ribbon. Must be the least lucky horseshoe ever.

God knows what must have happened to the poor horse that once wore it."

"Perhaps it belonged to Shergar. I'm afraid I threw away that horseshoe, so it couldn't ruin anyone else's life."

I notice that Ruth is trying to suppress a yawn, so I give up on my plans to tell her what happened with John earlier, and suggest we call it a night.

After Ruth has gone, I think about Mark. I used to hate him, but he was always there at key moments of my life, and I relied on him so much when I was little – he was the only one who understood what it was like living with Mummy. The only one I could properly talk to about her. I haven't seen him for ages. He never gets in touch now. I wonder why he has suddenly disappeared. I could do with talking to him; I feel that maybe now I could even tell him what really happened at the wedding. I reckon he would know what I should do.

I shut my eyes tight and try to summon him to me, like I used to in times of need when I was younger. But there is no knock on the door, no ringing phone, no ping of a text. Mark has abandoned me and I don't blame him – what was there to keep him here, once Mummy had gone?

Mark was the only person who told me not to marry Conrad, but many others must have had their doubts. It must have been obvious to everyone that we would never last.

Confession, Part Six

By the time I got to twenty-nine I was desperate to marry Conrad. I had been out with him for seven years, but it was clear that he was never going to propose. Whenever the subject of marriage came up, usually because I introduced it, Conrad would expound on why marriage was a convention that nearly always destroyed relationships. Also, it often preceded having children, and Conrad definitely did not want children. He called people with kids "breeders" and said it was selfish and egotistical, not to mention environmentally disastrous, to have children.

I think part of me thought that by marrying Conrad, I would be cementing our relationship; part of me knew that he was not fully committed to me, and I needed that commitment. So I badgered and harangued and nagged.

One Sunday morning we were sitting up in bed, the Sunday papers squashing our legs with their weight. It was impossible to read them all, so I always just read the magazine supplements. I wasn't reading this Sunday; I wanted to talk about getting married again: "It is so difficult us not being married. I can't keep pretending to my mother that we don't live together. I'm sick of her telling me that I'm becoming a crusty old spinster. Also, I'm fed up with living with you, whilst running my own flat, too."

"It doesn't cost you anything," replied Conrad, "as that cow Skye lives there."

It was a bit of a mystery to me why Skye had wanted to rent my flat – it was hardly handy for her job in Central London. When I had mentioned that I was looking for a tenant, she'd jumped at the chance. Mind you, she was never there that often, as she was always being offered beds to sleep in in hotels in the centre of town. None of the rock stars and film starts she interviewed, it seemed, could resist her. Especially the married ones.

"I'd like to sell the flat, and I'd like us to have our own place that we buy together. I don't like feeling like your lodger. I want to feel like your wife. I want to be your wife.

Call me old-fashioned, but I want you to declare to the world that you love me and want to be with me."

"You are old fashioned."

I turned back the duvet and got out of bed, stomping out of the room and into the living room. I sank down on one of the designer chrome-and-black leather chairs.

Conrad followed me and knelt next to me. *Ooh,* I thought, *perhaps this is it. Perhaps he is going to ask me now, at last!* He didn't.

He said: "You do know how much I love you don't you, Grace?"

I replied: "Then marry me."

Conrad sighed, then surprised me by saying: "Okay."

That was how I ungraciously proposed to Conrad and that was how he ungraciously accepted. He made no pretence that he was thrilled with the idea because he was worried that things would change between us. He refused to get drawn into any wedding preparations, although he insisted we could not get married in church and that it had to be a small wedding.

There was one part of the whole wedding malarkey he was keen on, though: having a luxury holiday (which he refused to call a honeymoon). His parents had offered to pay, which meant we could afford a luxury resort anywhere in the world.

Conrad was in need of a break because he was over-worked. He was losing weight and his suits were beginning to hang off him. When he came home from work each evening, shattered from the long hours plus a long commute, I would do all I could to recharge his batteries. I would make sure the flat was welcoming, healthy meals were prepared, juice was freshly squeezed, and I would offer to follow dinner with a massage, which I hoped would lead to sex. But he was so tired that he usually fell asleep before we got that far.

Things were not going well at the TV station. There had been cutbacks and there were more threats of redundancy. Skye had been let go six months before. She was now working as a celebrity columnist at a London paper, which she said was more work for less money. Her job was basically partying every night and then filing copy in the early hours of the morning.

Conrad said Skye had actually been fired for being unprofessional. Her time-keeping was awful, and there were complaints that in some live interviews she was slurring and acting in inappropriate ways. It was the time-keeping and slurring that were the problem – acting inappropriately had always been her thing.

One rare weekday night when she wasn't working and was planning to stay in my flat, she offered to make me dinner. When I turned up at eight o'clock, I was disappointed to find that "dinner" consisted of crisps, not even posh ones, and red wine. I turned down the vodka shots, which were the dessert.

"Oh come on, Grace, join me, don't be such a boring fart."

"I can't," I said, "I don't want to get drunk."

"Why ever not? What's good about being sober?"

"One, I can drive home; two, I won't feel crap in the morning; three—"

"Three, you're a sad, sad, sad, saddo." When Skye started repeating herself, it was time to leave. She wasn't happy about me going, and she begged me to stay the night. She hated my choosing to be with Conrad rather than her.

"Don't go, we could find somewhere to go dancing. We could do a few lines of coke to wake us up."

"You could do with going to bed, too, Skye. You're pushing yourself too far. If you carry on like this, you could lose this job, too. Not to mention the fact that you're probably killing yourself."

"Good," she said, "the sooner I am dead, the better."

I didn't take her seriously. After all, she was off her head, as usual. Like that time she told me that Conrad was a serial philanderer.

It was hard to know what to believe with Skye. I'm not even sure she believed all the stories she told – she was such a fantasist, she would have convinced herself that everything she said was true.

Although she slept with a fair few famous people, she couldn't have slept with all the ones she told me about. Richard Gere? Mick Jagger? Sting? Harrison Ford? Johnny Depp? I don't think so.

And when you knew she had slept with someone, or come close to it, as she did with Adam, she would often deny it afterwards. As proud as she was of having sex with the rich and famous, she was as ashamed if she had sex with someone she thought was a "nobody".

Knowing her history of stealing boyfriends, I was half-expecting her to make a move on Conrad. I wasn't overly concerned; I thought I knew Conrad well and had no fears that he would be tempted by Skye.

When they started working for the same TV company, I was waiting to hear that Skye had tried it on with Conrad at an office party or something, but Conrad claimed never to be in the same room as Skye.

According to Skye, they spoke all the time. She told me how close they had grown when I went out for cocktails with her one evening in Soho, in a small underground bar underneath a picture gallery. It was full of media darlings –

Skye loved it. This particular night, Skye regaled me with story after story of the funny things Conrad said to her. I asked her when they got to see each other.

"Oh all the time, Grace – it is such a small company, we are like one, big family. Most of use end up in the pub for lunch each day."

I could imagine Grace in the pub, but not Conrad; he liked to go to the gym at lunch time.

Then Skye looked down and started tearing pieces of her paper napkin.

"Actually, Grace, there is something I have to tell you."

I waited to hear one of her stories, and like clockwork, Skye's eyes started to well up, which was a sure-fire sign that she was lying. I never let on that I thought Skye made up half the stories she told me, as usually I enjoyed hearing her tales. I suspected, rightly, that this story was not going to be such a fun ride.

"This is very difficult to say ..."

"Then perhaps you shouldn't tell me," I said, knowing this probably was not an option.

"You have to know this, Grace, because it affects you. You should know what Conrad is getting up to behind your back."

Here we go, I thought.

"Whenever he can, even if we're just passing in the corridor, if no one else is around, he always comes right up to me, presses himself against me. I always push him away. I have found out from some others in the company that Conrad has a reputation for doing this – it isn't just me he targets."

"If that's true, why doesn't anyone report him to HR? Get him sacked for sexual harassment?"

Skye used another of her dramatic tactics: she covered

her face with her hands and leant forwards, shaking slightly as if crying. "He scares us so much!"

As if. I had no sympathy for Skye, but I was feeling sorry for myself wasting time with this hammy, drunk actress. Why did I do it to myself? The answer I always came up with was that I was worried about Skye. She looked to be heading towards a breakdown – her drinking was getting worse and her fantasies were getting out of control.

Skye didn't have many people to look out for her. Her mum had moved to the States, as had many in the commune she used to live in. They now lived in a much larger community, part of a movement that sounded madder than Scientology to me. Her only other friend was Justin, whom we had lived with at university. But Justin did not protect Skye; quite the opposite – he positively encouraged her wild excesses.

The lies that Conrad told me were much harder to spot. He was drunk about as often as Skye was sober; he hated losing control. I did, nevertheless, see him the worse for wear a few times. Once was just after he started his television job. At the end of his first week, he went out for an after-work drinks do. This was not his style, despite what Skye made out, as he generally did not like to socialise with colleagues. But he said he had to go for drinks this time in order to get to know the team.

He got home just before four am. I had been worried and furious in equal measure before he got home. I had expected a text or call to let me know he was going to be so late. When he eventually came back, he was so contrite, I couldn't stay cross. He threw open the bedroom door and stumbled in, stinking of beer and cigarette smoke and moving about extra noisily. He kept saying "ssshhh" or "sorry" as he crashed into another piece of furniture, eventually landing with a thump on the bed.

"Sorry!" he said again.

I sat up and turned on the bedside light. He was lying face down on the bed half undressed, just wearing a white shirt and boxers. He pushed himself up onto his elbows and looked at me.

"I really am so, so, sorry," he said, before falling back down flat on his face.

"It's okay," I said as I was so relieved to have him home. I was about to turn off the light when I realised that Conrad was crying. I had never seen him cry before. The whole bed gently shook with the rhythm of his quiet sobs.

"What on earth is wrong?" I stroked his shoulders.

He kept on crying. Then, after a while, he said: "It was such a stupid evening. I hate myself. I should never have drunk so much. I'm pathetic. I didn't want to go to those places ... Why am I so weak? Why didn't I just come home to you?"

He seemed to be making a huge deal out of one drunken night out. He told me that his night of shame had entailed going to seedier and seedier bars, ending in a lap dancing club. He hated that sort of thing.

"I don't deserve you, Grace. I can't be the person you want me to be."

"I don't want you to be anyone but yourself. Everyone gets drunk sometimes, you've only been to a strip club. I'm no angel, I'm sure I have done worse."

"No, you haven't. You don't have it in you. Hold me, Grace. Save me."

Conrad started crying again, so I put my arms around him.

Conrad kept repeating: "Please don't leave me. Please don't go."

Next day, Saturday, it was if the night before had never happened. When Conrad got up around ten, he was his usual self. I cooked him a fried breakfast. Afterwards, he kissed me on the cheek and said: "Sorry about last night." Then we went to Sainsbury's to do our weekly shop.

Chapter Seven

ELECTRIC SIGN DISTRACTS DRIVERS AND MAY CAUSE CRASH

By Grace O'Neill

An electronic information sign promoting the Dashford Dash,
an annual 10-mile cross-country run that supports many local

Wednesday, 10 July 1996

I wake up with toothache. I have been having a few nagging twinges lately, but this is a pain that demands serious painkillers. I hate going to the dentist, so I hope this is something temporary. Perhaps I have some sort of infection? My throat feels a bit sore – maybe I need antibiotics. Not that I can bear going to the doctor either.

There is only one cat to feed this morning, Blake. Miro must be out hunting, as it's a nice day. When I'm in the bathroom I try to see if my throat looks red in the mirror, but I can't tell. Instead, I notice something else that gives me a nasty turn. I see that I have some grey hairs. I can see at least five sprouting from my parting. What am I going to do? I have never dyed my hair in my life, apart from spraying in some Crazy Colour when I was seventeen. Shall I start dying it now? This is a burning issue I will have to discuss with Ruth later.

I can still chew, despite the pain in my mouth, and around mid-morning I'm tucking into a Danish at my desk when the phone rings. Trying desperately to swallow quickly so that I can speak, I pick up on the fourth ring.

"Hello, is this Grace O'Neill?"

"Mmhh." Another swallow. "Yes, Grace speaking."

"This is Jenny May – I was driving that bus involved in the accident?"

"Oh hello, Jenny, how are you?"

"Much better, thanks, I'm back driving now."

"So glad to hear that. How can I help?"

"I saw that woman again this morning on the bridge. The one I saw at the accident."

Jenny continues: "I knew it was her – she had the same bright shopping trolley; I just knew it was her the minute I caught sight of her. I stopped the bus, then jumped down to speak to her, quickly mind, as the cars behind weren't too happy. I expect my passengers were none too impressed neither. But I had to say something to her. I must have scared her something horrible, because she started crying, poor dear. Anyway, there's no way she could have pushed that poor man over. She's a tiny frail thing. Don't think so much pulls that shopping trolley as it pushes her. I told her she should go to the police and give a statement, though. Just thought you'd want to know."

"Thank you, Jenny, I really appreciate it."

"I almost didn't call you, but I don't want you tracking down that old lady and interviewing her. I think it would be the death of her. It wouldn't be right and I'd feel responsible for hurting her, as well as that poor guy on the bike."

"Don't worry," I say, "I won't be writing any more stories about the sad accident. I'm glad you managed to speak to the lady. I'm even more glad that you're back at work."

Mystery solved, I think after putting down the phone.

My nagging tooth makes it hard for me to concentrate, so I give in and call the dentist to make an appointment. I don't think it merits an emergency appointment, so I can't get to see my dentist for two more weeks, but I am in no rush to see him, so that suits me fine.

When I get home, there is still no sign of Miro. Blake seems happier, if anything – not bothered at all. Somehow, I expect him to be a bit sad and worried about Miro, because, like any self-respecting cat owner, I imbue the furry creature with human emotions. I myself am so worried about Miro that I sit down at the kitchen table and burst into tears. Crying, as I know better than anyone, does not solve anything, so I go upstairs to the study and create a Missing Cat poster.

I find a picture of Miro that makes my heart ache. There is handsome, and then there is ridiculously handsome. As well as pasting the picture into the poster, I type that a reward is on offer.

I print out ten A4 posters before I text Ruth.

Ruth texts back: *"Come over for dinner."*

I'm not hungry and I want to be at home in case Miro turns up, so I reply: *"Thanks, but not up to it. Coffee soon though."*

Miro does not turn up the next day, or the day after.

At three pm on Saturday, I get a call. The voice sounds warm, an older woman.

"Are you the lady that has lost a white, fluffy cat? With brown ears?"

"Yes, that's me." *Pease don't say anything bad, please don't tell me you have just seen his body ...*

"I think I have some good news for you, dear."

Hallelujah! Miro is alive! The woman on the phone, whose name is Iris, found Miro stuck up a tree in the park. She heard mewing and eventually spotted him, and asked a nice young man passing by to get him down. It took a while – jeans were torn and swear words were uttered – but Miro was recovered and wrapped up tightly in a cardigan. Iris then popped him in her shopping basket and took him back to her house. Miro must have been exhausted if he let himself be wrapped up like that.

Iris lives just a few streets away in a quiet cul-de-sac I have never gone down before. Her house is a small 1960s bungalow that an estate agent would describe as "having potential". I carry my empty cat basket up the front path, which is a veritable death trap with uneven paving stones that are cracked and wobbly and nearly trip me up several times. The front garden is too overgrown to be called charming, and the gloss paintwork on the door and window frames is faded and peeling.

The woman who opens the front door looks to be around eighty, with long black frizzy hair that gives her a witch-like appearance. Perhaps I shouldn't colour my hair if this is what mine could like one day. Iris is tiny, a good few inches less than five foot – hardly a person at all. I feel like the Incredible Hulk as I stand in front of her. A cat darts past us, out of the house into the garden. Not Miro, but a black cat. Her familiar, I guess.

"You must be Iris," I say. "You found my cat?"

Iris gives me a big smile and instantly looks ten years younger and much less creepy. She invites me in: "I'll take you to him straight away, dear, you must be desperate to see him. He is much stronger now, as I have fed him. I have put him in a cat carrier where he is quite safe and can't run away.

I rush up to the cat basket on the floor in the kitchen and crouch down. There is Miro looking sheepish. Not just because he is white and fluffy, but because he looks nervous, not his usual self at all. I open up the gate of the basket and reach in to pick him up. He shrinks back as though he doesn't know who I am. I try not to feel insulted. How can he be like this with me? His most favourite person in the world?

Holding him firmly under one arm, I open up the door of my cat basket and gently ease him inside. Iris asks if I would like to stay for a cup of tea.

"Thanks so much, but I had better get this boy home. I am so grateful to you – I can't tell you how much I have missed him." I reach into my back trouser pocket and pull out an envelope which has fifty pounds in cash in it as a reward. I hold it out to her.

"No, dear, there's no need for that. I'm glad I could help."

I insist, and reluctantly Iris takes the envelope. Judging from the state of the house, she could do with some extra money. There is a strong smell of cat litter, t a dirty cat litter tray on the floor by the back door, plus a few cat bowls dotted around with drying cat food remains in them.

I'm affected by Iris and her house. They are like a warning to me of how I could end up.

When I get Miro back to my more salubrious kitchen, I open the door of the cat basket and wait for him to leap out, ecstatic to be home. This doesn't happen. Instead, he edges out slowly and begins, cautiously, to explore his own habitat. Minutes after this, he is out in the garden, eyeing up the birds.

I call Ruth to tell her that I have Miro back, and describe Iris and her sad house.

"That is so freaky!" says Ruth. "That is the same woman who found Boris."

That is freaky. "What are the chances of that?" I ask.

"It can't be a coincidence," replies Ruth. "Neither of our cats has ever got lost before, and then they both go missing within weeks of each other and get kidnapped by a witch. And that story about asking a young man to rescue your cat just doesn't make sense. As if anyone would be able to climb a tree and then climb down again holding a cat!"

"What do you think we should do?"

"*We* shouldn't do anything," says Ruth. "But *you* could try being a proper investigative reporter for a change. Check her out. I bet our cats are not the only ones she has claimed to have found through lucky chance."

I promise Ruth that I will find a way to get to the truth. Not sure how, I will sleep on it. Or rather, toss and turn and think about it when I'm not obsessing over my usual worries.

Confession, Part Seven

It is nice to be loved, but being smothered by love is another matter. Both my mother and Skye loved me too much. I loved them, too – I loved them to death as it happens – but I also hated them.

When I was ill and unable to run away, I felt the full force of their devotion. It seemed to me that Mummy loved it when I was sick. The sicker, the better.

If I came down in the morning looking peaky, she would rush to get the glass thermometer and stick it uncomfortably under my tongue.

"Oh dear, oh dear," she would mutter if it was a fraction over the norm. "Back to bed with you!"

I hated being sick. It meant at least one day shut up in my room with the curtains drawn. As Mummy said, you had to starve a fever, and she would ration me to broth and hot water with Lemsips if my temperature was particularly high. I couldn't go downstairs to watch TV, and if she caught me listening to my prized radio-clock alarm, she would switch it off. I was either horribly bored and hungry, or horribly ill. I'm not sure which was worse.

Mummy kept me prisoner like that for as long as she possibly could, cutting me off from school, my friends, and the outside world. All bad influences in her view. She couldn't stop me seeing Mark. He would creep in from time to time, but usually he would make fun of me and leave quickly as I was "no fun" when I was sick.

Skye wasn't always that interested in me when I was ill, but when we were at university, if she was between boyfriends, she would become overbearingly motherly if I was not feeling my best.

There was the time I was having problems with my wisdom tooth coming through. After a few weeks of me moaning on about the pain and begging Skye for her extra-strong painkillers, she took me in hand.

She made an appointment for me with her dentist, who

she said was one of the most attractive men in Leeds. That was of no interest to me; all I wanted was a dentist with unending patience and a talent for administering anaesthetic. Skye came with me to the dental surgery and it soon became obvious her reason for coming was not because of me, but because she had set on sights on Mr Roister, the gorgeous dentist. He was married, too, which was always a turn-on for Skye. I was in a right state in the waiting room, so Skye passed me a couple of small yellow tablets and told me to take them. They were the first Diazepam I ever tried.

In the end, I had to go to Leeds General Hospital to have the tooth removed under general. For some reason, my needing an operation made Skye go all maternal. She got our flatmate Justin to take me to the hospital and collect me afterwards. She even made me soup. She and Justin fussed over me as if I were their little girl. It was like they were acting parts in some dreadful 1960s sitcom.

I spent a few days lying under a blanket on the sofa. I wasn't really that ill, but it was a treat to be allowed to be an invalid whilst watching TV and eating comfort food. Skye spent hours by my feet, talking, talking, talking.

"Oh, it's so nice to spend time with you, Grace, just us two. I feel we're so close, we know everything there is to know about each other."

I didn't point out that as she was doing all the talking; although I knew a lot about how she was thinking and feeling, she knew very little about me.

Chapter Eight

Monday, 15 July 1996

I have another animal corpse to dispose of. I feel like an undertaker sometimes as well as an executioner. The body is that of a squirrel. I can't believe that a squirrel could be stupid enough to be killed by one of my cats, but the evidence on the kitchen floor by the catflap suggests otherwise. I have put two bells on each cat's collar and I now resolve to get some more bells. My cats need sirens on them and flashing lights to warn their prey, but I have to be realistic.

After burying the squirrel, I go for a run. Ruth and I are managing to go further each time, whilst our breaks for collapsing and wheezing are getting smaller. We can run for twenty minutes without stopping now. Then we walk for a bit and sprint home. I say "sprint" because it feels like we're running very, very fast. Being good at maths, Ruth works out that our average speed is a twelve-minute mile – not fast, but a miracle as far as I'm concerned.

I get to work on time as I don't want John having another go at me. Being punctual, however, is not enough to make him look happy. I try to cheer him up by telling him that I'm working on a story that could be major.

"Don't tell me it is about one of your cats." How does he know? "I'm not sure our readers are ready for that level of excitement."

"My cat does come into this story," I confess, "but wait until you hear how."

I tell John about Iris, the cat stealer, but John isn't impressed. "Two missing cats, hmm. No matter how I spin that in my head, I can't see it making the front page. Or any other page."

I don't let John's negativity stop me. I will check this out. I start by calling Iris to tell her I'm working on a feature about how she rescued my cat and I'd like to pop over to take a photograph.

"Oh no, I don't want to be in the paper," she says.

"We have so many bad news stories in Dashford," I lie, "It would be refreshing to have a story with a happy ending for a change. Please think about it. I could bribe you with a cake from the new bakery in the high street."

"There's no need for that, dear. I'm quite capable of

baking my own cakes. Why don't you come over for a cup of tea, though, and we can talk about it. I would love to hear how your cat is getting on. What's his name again?"

"Miro."

"Oh yes, such a handsome chap. Come round when you're passing by and I'll put the kettle on. I don't go out much these days, I am home most of the time."

"Okay, Iris, I'll call you later in the week to let you know I am on my way."

"That will be a wonderful treat for me," says Iris, which makes me feel bad for planning to expose her as a catnapper.

John comes over to my desk to find out how I'm getting on. I don't mention the Iris story again, but I tell him about the rumour that a Marks and Spencer store may be opening. I also promise to call the local sign makers to see if they are working on any signs that could be construed as controversial. This is John's favourite type of story and I see his eyes light up.

John has not tried to ask me out again, although he is still being unnatural when he is around me. I'm hoping that normal service will resume soon.

Another visitor to my desk today is Charlotte, the new sub. Today, her shoes are far more sensible – flat ballet pumps. She tells me that as well as subbing, she can also write features, so I must feel free to ask for her help if I need it.

After work, I head to Ruth's for supper and to continue talking about my disastrous wedding.

We eat roast chicken with salad and garlic bread. The boys are making the house shake as they thump and crash around upstairs "sleeping". Graham is out at the local pub quiz, with John, I assume.

Ruth and I settle down after dinner on her blue Habitat sofa, which I'm reassured to see is in a worse state than the Ercol settee I have. Like my settee, the cushions are lumpy, and it is decorated with chocolate and wine stains, with a fair sprinkling of cat fur on top. Ruth puts on a CD to get my mind back to the wedding day. The track that comes on is the song that serenaded us as we walked out of the Register Office. "Love Cats" by The Cure.

The wedding party, around thirty of us in all, then piled onto a coach which took us to a wharf close to Kingston Bridge. Conrad and I stood by the gangplank to welcome everyone as they stepped onto the riverboat where we were holding the reception.

So far so good, the wedding day was on track. Everyone, not counting Mummy, looked happy. Apart from being disappointed that we didn't get married in church, Mummy was cross because it was such a small wedding. She had wanted to invite all our Irish relatives over, but Conrad had been firm about keeping the numbers down.

We did have a few of the Irish contingent there. Mummy's sister Maggie, my favourite auntie, was one of these. It was Auntie Maggie who cornered me just as the finger buffet was being laid out.

"Sweet girl, I need to talk to you about Mary."

We had quite a few Marys in the family, but I knew she meant my mother.

"Of course, shall we go outside? There is a small deck at the back of the boat where we can be alone."

"Good idea, dearest child," said Auntie Maggie. "I don't want Mary to see we're having a private chat or she'll start worrying."

"You go outside first then and I'll join you when Mummy's not watching."

Five minutes later, Auntie Maggie and I were sitting by the rail, the wind whipping our hair. This made me keen to keep the conversation short. Auntie Maggie got straight to the point, taking my hand before she spoke, which should have made me realise she had bad news.

"Your mother is dying."

I heard the words, I knew what they meant, but I couldn't believe them.

"Sorry? Mummy is dying? How do you know? What do you know? Why hasn't she told me?"

"I'm so sorry to give you this news on your wedding day, but I didn't want to tell you over the phone, and when else would I get a chance to speak to you? Mary swore me to secrecy – she said she didn't want to ruin the early days of your marriage. But I know if it were me, I would want to know my own mother was dying. There will be things you will want to say to her, you will want to at least say goodbye."

"You're making it sound like she could drop down any minute ... What is wrong with Mummy?"

"She went to the doctor because she has been having dizzy spells and problems with her memory. She thought maybe she was getting dementia, but a brain scan showed a tumour. I'm afraid it is inoperable."

"How long has she got?"

"Not long. She says she doesn't want any chemotherapy or radiotherapy. It won't be long. Weeks probably, maybe months."

As the news sank in, I covered my face with my hands and started crying. Auntie Maggie passed me a tissue and patted my arm. She stayed quiet; I kept weeping. "There, there," she murmured. "There, there."

The door close to us opened out and Conrad's head

appeared. When he saw the state I was in, he came outside and shut the door behind him.

"Regretting marrying me already?" he quipped. Conrad never knew what do with himself when he saw me cry.

When I didn't reply, he turned to Auntie Maggie: "Whatever it is you have told her about me, I swear to you it isn't true!"

As his flippant remarks were falling on deaf ears, Conrad sat down on the other side of me, put his arm around my shoulders, and said gently: "Grace, sweetheart, it's nothing too serious, is it?"

I sniffed and shook my head. "Sorry, Conrad, I think all the emotion of the day is getting to me. Don't worry, I'll be okay in a minute."

Conrad stood up and leant down to speak to Auntie Maggie quietly. "Can I ask you a special favour, Maggie? Please can you help Grace get herself together? It is time for the speeches, and everyone is waiting for her."

Ruth interrupts me: "I remember getting so anxious about the speech I was making. I wanted to get it over and done with so that I could start hitting the champagne."

I looked at Ruth. "I never thanked you for your beautiful speech," I say. "It must have been such an effort writing it and then delivering it so perfectly. You must have rehearsed and rehearsed. I should have thanked you. I'm an awful friend."

"You're always telling me what a dreadful friend you are, and right now you're a completely rubbish friend," says Ruth. "But I can forgive you for not thanking me for the speech, which, you're right, I spent ages rehearsing. After all, you had rather a lot to deal with after the wedding."

These words start me off. The usual tiresome weeping and wailing.

"Okay, that's enough for today," Ruth sighs. She doesn't try to comfort me; she has got so used to seeing me in this state. She gets up and puts a film on. "If you're going to keep crying, keep the noise down. I want to watch this."

The film is *Thelma and Louise*, which helps to cheer me up. Two women killing themselves – how come that is a feel-good movie?

Confession, Part Eight

Until I got married, I felt that how I looked was dictated by others to some extent. When I say others, I mean Mummy, Skye, and Conrad.

It started with Mummy policing the length of my hair for as long as she had the power to. The cutting of my hair in the summer was a ritual that lasted until I was well into my teens, when I flatly refused to let her touch my hair anymore. Mummy never took me to the hairdressers, as they were for hussies. She only once cut my hair when I was asleep; instead, she used to cut it in the kitchen. It was a job that lasted all of one minute.

On the first day of the summer holidays, Mummy would tie my hair back in a loose pony tail. Then she would sit me down on a wooden kitchen stool, get out the kitchen scissors, and a few snips later, my pony tail would be lying the on the black-and-white kitchen floor tiles. That was my yearly haircut. I would beg her not to do it each time, but she would give me that look. The one that meant she could see through me to my rotten core. It was severe and sympathetic at the same time.

She didn't beat me, well, not severely; she only slapped and spanked. Physical punishment was not her forte; she specialised in less obvious methods of chastisement.

First of all, there was the silent treatment. This could last up to a month. Once Daddy died, this became quite a frequent punishment. Often, I would never find out what I had done to make Mummy stop talking to me.

Another favourite was limiting my food. I think this was partly because Mummy didn't want me to get fat; she hated fat people and had always been on to Daddy about his weight.

Mummy was ingenious when it came to thinking up ways of stamping out the evil in me. When I was twelve, for example, I was once woken up by cold drops of water landing on my forehead.

I stared up to see Mummy leaning over me. "What are you doing?" I asked.

"Darling girl, I am sprinkling you with holy water, to get the demons out of you whilst you sleep. Just shut your eyes, my angel, and when you wake up, you will have all your natural sweetness and goodness restored."

I never found out what I had done that day for Mummy to think I was possessed with demons. The funniest of things could set her off. There was the time when I was ten and came home with a self-portrait I'd done at school. I was terribly proud of it and had won a school certificate for it. I showed it to Mummy and she stood still, gripping the paper whilst the blood drained from her face. Then her cheek began to quiver. "No, no, no," she muttered. She took the picture to the kitchen sink, grabbed some matches from beside the cooker, and set fire to it.

I was too shocked to say anything. Mummy turned round from the sink where the picture was burning and hissing as the water in the bottom of the sink put out the flames.

"It's alright, darling, I've got rid of it for you. It can't hurt you anymore."

"What are you talking about? The teachers said it was a good picture! I got a prize for it."

"I could see the devil in its eyes. But don't worry, it's gone to hell now where it belongs."

Concerned at all times that I might set off one of her irrational destructive acts, I became adept at appearing to be a model child. At home, I wore no makeup, modest clothing, and tried to be good. Once I was outside the home, I tried to establish my own identity. I'd hitch up my skirt, put on lipstick, and generally act as bad as I could. Which, looking back, was not very bad at all.

I didn't realise quite what a good girl I was until I became friends with Skye. She took me in hand. She gave me makeovers where I would find it hard to breathe as half a can of hairspray was used to make sure my back-combed hair remained standing up high from my head. It was positively crispy when she was finished with it. She took scissors and sandpaper to distress my jeans, so that they were more holes than material.

Before we went out, she often ordered me back to the bathroom to apply more eyeliner. I was her dressing-up doll whom she spent more time undressing than dressing. I don't mean she got me naked – there was nothing obviously sexual about her motives. But when it came to getting dressed, her motto was definitely "less is more"; she preferred a look that was less about clothing and more about the body.

Conrad's attitude to my appearance was also somewhat proprietorial. Not long after we got together, he took me shopping. His favourite store was Harvey Nichols, whereas I had always been a Top Shop girl. Conrad liked to treat me to clothes that cost ridiculous amounts of money. Silk shirts, tailored trousers, and skirts in fine, light wools. Then there was the underwear. Conrad adored lingerie, especially corsets. I refused to wear these during the day, as they weren't exactly comfortable. Apart from my wedding day, when I squeezed myself into an oyster-silk corset I knew Conrad would love. It was a shame he never saw me in it.

Chapter Nine

Tuesday, 16 July 1996

After the cathartic evening at Ruth's last night, I sleep right through until six am, waking up feeling almost refreshed. No run today and, as it is such a warm morning, I take my breakfast outside into my overgrown garden and settle on one of the white plastic chairs at the white plastic table. Well, they were white once, and there are still a few white patches under the green and black splodges of mould. I have fried tomatoes on toast liberally coated with butter. My margarine days are over.

That is what I think until I visit Iris. I phone her at lunchtime to warn her I plan to call in after work. When I arrive, I find that she has gone to the trouble of making me afternoon tea.

After opening the front door, Iris throws her bird-like arms around me as if I'm her most favourite person it the world. It feels strange to hold such a small, fragile person. She smells of lavender and is wearing a dress that is far too big for her. It looks like it was bought from Laura Ashley in the 1970s – brown cotton covered with sprigs of white flowers.

"Hello dear, I'm so delighted you have come for tea. I have laid it out for us in the conservatory."

The conservatory turns out to be a lean-to that is barely attached to the back of the kitchen – a few hard kicks is all that it would take to flatten it. It has a corrugated Perspex roof covered in green fungus and dirt, so that it doesn't let much of the July sunshine in. There is a small, round table covered with a white linen table cloth, embroidered blue-bells decorating its scalloped edge. On top of the table are delicate china plates. On one plate is a large pile of bread and margarine (I only realise it is margarine after I bite into a piece, which is a bit of a disappointment). On another plate is a Victoria sponge, obviously homemade. My sore tooth throbs as I look at the cake, as if to remind me that sugar isn't good for me.

"Iris, you shouldn't have gone to so much trouble," I say.

"It's not often I get the chance to make a fuss of some-one. What would you like to drink, tea or coffee?"

"Tea, please, Iris. You have to drink tea with a Victoria sponge."

When we have our china cups full of tea in front of us, Iris looks at me with her blue eyes. I notice how clear they are, and I hope my eyes are as bright when I get to her age. If I get to her age. Iris says: "I hope you aren't still planning to write a story about me."

I say: "I won't write about you if you don't want me to" – which is not a promise any self-respecting journalist should ever make – "but I would love to interview you about your uncanny knack for finding lost cats."

"What do you mean?"

"Well, you found my Miro and you also found Boris, my friend Ruth's cat."

Iris gives a little shudder: "Don't remind me about that nasty cat Boris. I know all cats are God's creatures, but that Boris was a menace. Quite scared the life out of Mable," she says and points at a black cat snoozing in the sun on the lino floor in the corner. "I have to admit, you are right about me having a knack for finding cats. I'm not sure I'd want you writing about in the local news, though, dear."

"How many cats have you found, do you think?"

Iris surprises me by jumping up and out of her chair. She is nifty, is Iris: "Wait here and I will show you exactly how many cats I have found!" And she darts out of the room.

Soon, Iris is back and under her arm there is a bulging scrapbook.

I move the plates and cups so there is room for her to place it on the table. "These," she declares, "are all the cats I have found over the years."

The scrapbook has a thin cardboard cover and some of the pages have come loose. There are also larger bits of paper sticking out of it. I'm worried the whole thing will disintegrate when I open it. I carefully turn the first page, where there is a sheet of A4 paper sellotaped showing a photo of a fluffy kitten –a "Lost" poster. There is no date on the poster, but it looks old, with the paper yellowing. I turn the page: there is another lost cat poster. And it goes on. Page after page of posters, looking less and less faded towards the end of the scrapbook. There are fat cats, fluffy cats, ginger cats, black cats, pedigree cats. Cats walking, cats sitting, cats asleep. On the last two pages there is the poster with Boris's picture on it, followed by the one I made for Miro.

"Are you saying you have found all these cats?" I ask, trying not to sound horrified. This is weird.

Iris replies, her eyes shining with pride: "Oh yes, whenever I see a missing cat poster go up, I make it my business to try and find him. I can't bear to think of those poor owners, bereft because they don't know what has happened to their beloved cat. I know what it is like to lose someone you love."

"But you can't always find the cats, surely?"

"No dear, I wish I could. Lots of the cats will have got run over, and there is nothing I can do about that. I'm afraid there are far more posters I have thrown away than I have kept."

"How did you manage to track down all these cats?"

"Well, your Miro was not the only cat I have found in a tree. I always check trees – the cats can be hard to spot – but I have had years of practice. Also, I have a sixth sense. I just know when there is a cat nearby. It helps that when I am on a hunt, I carry a tin of sardines. Cats can smell a sardine a long way off – they can't resist a sardine."

If this is true, this is quite a story. I'm sure John will eat his words when he hears about this; it is definitely feature material. But no matter how much I cajole Iris, I can't persuade her to let me write about her.

I give up pestering her about starring in the *Dashford Times* and compliment her on the garden. It is overgrown, but has a wild charm about it, similar to my own garden.

Iris takes me outside to take a look around.

"I used to love gardening," says Iris, "but I don't have the strength to do as much as I'd like to. When I do cut it back, I get left with piles of cuttings I don't know what do with. You can only have so many compost heaps."

"I could come over and give you a hand," I offer. "I don't know much about gardening, but I can chop and take away a few bags of garden waste for you."

"Oh no, I couldn't ask you to do that."

I offer again, assuring her it is no trouble, and eventually Iris agrees to let me come over one Sunday to help her do some pruning and tidying.

I am inept at looking after my own garden, yet here I'm offering to help do someone else's. What is my motive, I wonder? Am I hoping to get her to agree to the feature? I'm not usually so dedicated to my work. Perhaps there is something about Iris and her home that is calling me to come back ...

Confession, Part Nine

As I try to get to grips with my past, my doomed relationships with Mark, Mummy, Skye, and Conrad, I can see they were all full of dishonesty and pretence. With Mark, I never could know what was going on in his head and vice versa. I never let Mummy and Skye know how much I felt suffocated by them. When it came to Conrad, I now know he kept his true self hidden from me. He was the one person I was really "myself" with, but he was unable to be "his self" with me.

I should have taken more notice of the clues that he wasn't committed to spending the rest of his life attached to me.

It wasn't just that he didn't want to get married or that he took no interest in any of the wedding plans. For example, when I asked him where he wanted our wedding list, he replied: "Nowhere". He said we didn't need any more stuff.

Conrad shared nothing with me. There was nothing that was "ours". I wonder if he ever intended on us becoming a team. He was clear about not wanting children. The flat we lived in was his flat. I assumed we would buy a home together after the wedding, but whenever I raised the subject, Conrad prevaricated, saying we could sort it out after we'd got the wedding over with.

Why did it never occur to me that he just wasn't that into me? He was always declaring his love for me, buying me presents, spoiling me. But when it came down to it, he wasn't there. I mean, he literally wasn't there – we spent a lot of time apart.

Right from the start, Conrad and I hardly ever went on holiday together – the odd long weekend, yes, but never a trip lasting weeks, or even one week. Our two-week honeymoon would have been our longest trip away together. Conrad was often away at weekends – playing golf, shooting, skiing, or on a work trip. He also worked late, or went to the gym after work.

I didn't check up on him because, naively, I trusted him. Also, I enjoyed the freedom he gave me. I liked being in the flat on my own. I liked having days where I didn't speak to anyone. After having lived with Mummy and Skye, it was a blessed relief.

Not that I could completely escape them just because I didn't live with them.

Mummy liked me to go over for lunch every Sunday, and I often went alone as Conrad was usually busy. She used to call me most days, too, and was always asking me to pick her up items from the high street, as I so conveniently worked there. I think she just wanted to have an excuse to get me to drop in. When I did drop in, she would always have so much to tell me. She was full of conversation, but lacked enough people to share it with. I would much rather visit Mummy than have her visit me, as I didn't want her to know that I wasn't actually living in the flat I had bought.

One of Mummy's favourite topics was Christmas. She would start talking about this in June and would always be upset that Conrad was never free to join us, as Christmas was a Big Deal for Mummy. She cooked far too much food and got into a religious froth that meant she hardly slept at all over the festive period.

I used to say to Conrad that it would be nice to be together at Christmas, but he said he didn't want to leave his mother alone with his father. Apparently, one of his father's favourite Christmas pastimes was belittling his wife.

This meant that both Conrad and I put our mothers before each other. This would have changed once we got married, though, surely? Anyhow, I was too frightened about make a big deal about Christmas; I didn't want to seem too needy.

Skye, on the other hand, had no qualms about being needy. She used to beg me to spend Christmas with her. Her mother had moved to a commune in America, so she said she had nowhere to go. Whatever man she was seeing usually had a wife and Skye's only other close friend was our old flatmate Justin, who always went home to his own family in Edinburgh for Christmas and Hogmanay. Sometimes Skye would go with him, but I got the impression that his parents were as keen on Skye as my mother was.

Once, around four years ago now, a week before Christmas, Skye invited me over to my flat which she was renting, to watch her wrap presents. It did not sound like a fun evening, but by this point in our friendship, I no longer had any fun with Skye. I saw her out of duty.

As usual, when she opened the door she was noticeably drunk. She weaved into the lounge and slumped down on the orange IKEA armchair. I'd bought all my furniture from IKEA and then I never used it, as when I'd bought the flat I was practically staying at Conrad's full time. He insisted I buy my own place, though, as an "investment". As it happens, I just about broke even when I sold it. All that furniture was trashed by then, so I carted it all to the dump.

When I sat down on a contrasting blue armchair, I asked Skye where all the presents were she wanted to wrap. She said: "Oh, I haven't bought any."

"So why did you ask me to come over and watch you wrap them?"

"Because I need you with me. Anyway, I lied. I do have one special present. It is for you. Not much point wrapping it – you can have it now."

"I hope you haven't got me anything too extravagant, that would make me feel bad."

"I want you to feel bad. I want you to feel bad for not caring about me half as much as I care about you. For giving all your love to that stupid boyfriend of yours."

I did my best to appease her. "Of course I care about you, Skye, but our friendship is different from my relationship with Conrad. They are not mutually exclusive. Sometimes you make me think that you'd only be happy if I was single."

"I would be happier if you were single than with that bastard."

I sighed and tried to change the subject. "So when are you going to give me this amazing gift then?" I asked.

"I would like to wait until Christmas Day to give it to you, but as you're going to be with 'Mummy Dearest' I'll have to give it to you now. I don't know why you put that monster before me."

I felt like saying that if I saw Skye instead, then I would be simply exchanging one monster for another, but I bit my tongue.

"Come on then, Skye, show me my present! Sorry that I haven't brought yours." I did actually have a small gift for Skye in my bag, but was worried that it would be embarrassing to give her the lipstick I had bought her if she had got me something enormous. Granted, it was a Chanel lipstick, but still. I would just about have time to buy her something extra if her present was as extravagant as she was making out.

"Okay, I'm sure you will absolutely love it!" Skye jumped up, almost knocking over a ceramic lamp, and veered out of the room, tripping slightly on the edge of a rug as she left. "Close your eyes and hold out your hand!" she ordered when she returned.

I felt something cold and small drop into my hand.

"Open your eyes!"

I looked down to see what looked like an engagement ring. There was a small diamond neatly enclosed in a wide solid band of gold.

"Wow!" I said. "That's beautiful. It looks like a real diamond, and real gold."

"That's because it is real, silly. I wanted to get you something beautiful to represent our friendship. Something solid, that will last."

"It looks like an engagement ring."

"That is because it is an engagement ring. You're never going to get one from Conrad and a girl like you deserves to have a stunning engagement ring. So I got you one."

I didn't want to have an engagement ring, especially not from Skye. I did hope to marry Conrad, that was true, but I was not bothered about a ring. Jewellery had never been my thing.

"I can't accept it, Skye. It must have cost you a fortune. I can't afford to get you anything half as exquisite in return. I would feel bad keeping it." I held it out to her.

Skye took the ring.

"Hold out your hand," she commanded.

I held out my right hand.

"Your other hand!" said Skye.

"Why can't it go on my right hand?"

"Because then it wouldn't be so special. Hold out your left hand."

So I did. Skye then very slowly edged the ring onto my ring finger. It fitted perfectly.

"It looks gorgeous on you," said Skye.

I didn't know what to say. It was a lovely, simple ring. In the end, I mumbled "Thank you" and left it at that.

When Conrad saw it later that evening, he wasn't happy. "You have to stop seeing that woman," he said. "She is obsessed with you and you're encouraging her. Give back the ring and tell her you want nothing more to do with her."

"That's easy for you to say, Conrad," I said. "It isn't easy breaking up with a friend. Also, I worry about Skye. What if she did something stupid?"

"Who gives a monkey's? What is the point of Skye? What does she contribute to this planet apart from looking pretty? And that won't last much longer, the way she is destroying herself."

"That's a poor argument," I replied. "What do I contribute to the planet? I don't even look that pretty?"

Conrad gathered me in his arms. "You look beautiful. And you give plenty this world. You make me very happy, for one."

He always knew how to make me feel special with his weasel words.

Chapter Ten

Saturday, 20 July 1996

I feel pretty good for a Saturday. I have plans, which helps, and my toothache is only a slight nagging pain that has responded well to the aspirin I've taken alongside my morning coffee. No breakfast, as I'm running with Ruth and then we plan to have the full works at Franco's after.

When I knock on Ruth's door, there are crashes and screams emanating from the house, the usual twin play-fighting sound effects. Ruth answers, and the bags under her eyes look particularly bad, so I guess she didn't have a brilliant night's sleep.

"Thank God you're here to rescue me from this mayhem. I'm looking forward to running away. I just hope I have the strength and willpower to come back. Sometimes I envy you living alone."

"It's lonely," I reply.

"Oh don't give me that," says Ruth. "Why can't you feel sorry for me for a change?"

"Yes, you have a terrible life ... A fit, loving husband ... Two healthy kids ... Though I guess you do have a hideous cat."

"Don't you dare insult Boris. You have stepped over the line now."

I run down the path. "If you can catch me up, you can beat me up!"

It takes Ruth all of half a second to get level with me.

"So what's new?" she asks.

"I have news about that woman who rescued our cats – Iris," I say. I explain about going for tea and describe the scrapbook. And that I am going to help with Iris's garden.

Ruth stops running. I look back to see that she is standing looking cross, her hands on her hips. I stop running, too.

"I do *not* believe you!" says Ruth.

"What do you mean?" I ask. "Come on, we can argue about this and run at the same time." So we break into a slow jog, definitely a less-slow jog that we wouldn't have been able to manage a few weeks before.

"I just don't get you sometimes," Ruth continues. "First, there is the strange matter of you offering to do some gardening. If you want to garden, why not start with your own?"

"I'm planning to do my own garden, too," I explain. "I'm going to the garden centre this afternoon to pick up some plants. Visiting Iris has inspired me to do something with the—"

Ruth raises her voice, cutting me off: "But what I *really* can't understand is how you can be gullible enough to fall for Iris's stories about rescuing cats."

"You don't really think she steals them, do you?"

"Of course she bloody steals them! She obviously takes them before the cat posters go up. She keeps them, waits for the posters to appear, and then calls the devastated owners after a few days. She must do it for the reward money, or perhaps she's lonely and it's the only way she can entice stupid fools like you into her lair."

"If you got to know her," I say, "you would see what a sweetie she is. She went to such trouble making me tea. She doesn't seem like the devious type to me."

"That hardly fills me with confidence – you aren't the best judge of character. I hope she doesn't steal you next. I don't want to be putting up posters with your sad mug on it saying: 'Have you seen this woman? Goes by the name of Grace?'"

"How much reward would you offer to get me back?"

"Hmm, that's a good point. I may not be able to pay any reward. Shame. I'll miss you, Grace."

I give Ruth a light, playful punch. This is a mistake. Ruth then throws a playful punch back at me that knocks me clear off the footpath, sending me hurtling towards a tree.

When I have recovered and am running next to Ruth again, we drop the subject of Iris and start discussing whether we need sausages as well as bacon for breakfast. We decide that we do.

Less than an hour later, we're sitting at a corner table. I feel self-conscious being out in my sweaty state, devoid of makeup and with my hair tied back. I hope no one I know sees me. Ruth wakes me up from my vain ponderings by asking me to talk about the wedding again.

"Oh, must I? Can't we give it a rest? I don't think it is helping me."

"Well, something is helping. I have noticed that you're generally becoming a bit less of a miserable cow. But if you don't want to talk about the past right now, how about talking about your future?"

"What future?"

"You can't stay living like you do forever. As much as I love having you in the next street, don't you think it is about time you moved out of your family house?"

"I haven't got the energy to move right now."

"You just ran over four miles. How much energy do you need?"

"A lot more," I reply. "I need mental energy. I need to be able to imagine a new future for myself. Where would I go? What's the point of moving to somewhere else in Dashford? I would just be taking my problem with me. I am the problem."

Ruth sighs and looks up to the ceiling, as if she is studying something up there. I look up, but all I can see is plain, white plaster. Her gaze then comes back so that she is looking straight at me. She looks like she might cry. Oh dear.

"Your lethargy," she says, "your unwillingness to do something with your life is taking its toll on me. I can't solve your problems; all I can do is listen. But I can't keep listening to you forever, saying the same things again and again. I'm fed up with hearing your excuses about how your life is in ruins and you can never recover. You are young, you are healthy, you are eminently employable. Leave Dashford. Get a new life. And you definitely don't want to hear this, but you have to make up your mind about John, too. It is obvious you're circling around each other and it is becoming painful to watch. It is time to act rather than wallow!"

"I am doing something. Give me a break, Ruth. I'm running. I'm starting gardening. I'm helping an elderly neighbour ..."

"A nutcase neighbour. She certainly isn't a good excuse for staying here."

"You are a good excuse for staying here, Ruth," I say.

"I don't want to be your reason for staying – it puts too much pressure on me. I have my family to look after. It's not that I want you to leave; it's just that I think you need to get out of this place. Even if you and John get it together, you don't want to be sitting in the same office with him day in, day out."

I nod. "You're right. I should go. I just don't know where I could go."

"You're taking the first step, by considering leaving. That's all you have to do right now – think about changing things. Something will happen to help you decide where to go."

Later that day, something clicks into place in my head. My brother Mark ends up being the catalyst that helps me to decide what I need to do next. After an exhausting afternoon clearing out my garden, I sit on the settee with my laptop on the coffee table in front of me. I need to talk to Mark, so I begin a live email chat with him.

"How can I move on? And where should I move to?"

The reply comes: *"You know the answers to both of those*

*questions. What does your heart tell you? Listen. Really
listen."*

So I do. And I realise what my first step needs to be.

Two months after my wedding day, I became the last one
standing. No close family, no husband. I was living alone in
my childhood home, with no motivation to do anything to
the house apart from maintain it as simply as I could – a
shrine to my past. Everywhere I looked, there seemed to be
something to remind me of what I had lost. I managed to
throw away a few things, such as some of the framed
photographs on the upright piano. Conrad and me in Paris.
My graduation picture. The rest of the photographs I put in
the suitcase. I couldn't bear to see my parents looking at me,
bear to imagine the disappointment they would have in me.
Or the compassion which would have been even worse.

I have found all the sympathy I have had from Ruth, my
colleagues, old friends, and relatives unbearable. Eventually, the waves of sympathy stopped, and I was left here on
my own, where I could allow myself to be as miserable as I
wanted.

Now, I realise, I want to move on, and away.

I go to the computer and start typing. I email every
possible contact I can think of asking for freelance work,
and when I say every possible contact, that makes a total of
three: Emma, our last editorial assistant now at the London
glossy; Peter, who used to be chief sub and now works up in
Leeds at *The Yorkshire Mail*; and Michelle, a friend from
university who is a fashion editor for a trade magazine in
New York.

Then I realise I need to message Mark again. There is
one more question I need his help to answer. What to do
about my confused feelings about John. There is no reply.

Chapter Eleven

MOUSE DROPPINGS FOUND IN BISCUIT SELECTION TIN

By Grace O'Neill

You do not want to find that someone has beaten you to the best biscuits when you open up a new tin, you especially do not want to find evidence that a mouse has been there first. Yet this

Monday, 22 July 1996

Today is the day of the dreaded dentist appointment. As I assume my tooth problem is minor, I dose myself with just two milligrams of Diazepam to take the edge off my nervousness as I sit in the waiting room. This is nowhere near enough for the trauma that is about to befall me.

My dentist, Mrs Jefferson, has silver hair tied back so tightly in a bun that it gives her a slight facelift. She has never suggested that I call her by her first name. Mrs

Jefferson pokes around inside my mouth before taking an X-ray. Next, she delivers the bad news: my tooth needs to be removed. The good news, she says, is that she can do it straight away. Not good news at all, but I pretend to be brave and agree that it is a good idea to get it over and done with.

Mrs Jefferson injects me with so much local anaesthetic that my head feels as large as a watermelon. The torture begins. Unexpectedly, I hear a loud crack, so loud it sounds like a gun has been fired. Fired inside my head. I start to shake.

Mrs Jefferson and her dental assistant, Tess, try to calm me down. Tess holds my hand and Mrs Jefferson speaks softly as she explains that the worst is over, that the noise I heard was my tooth breaking, and that all I will have to endure next is maybe another loud sound and a bit of tugging. All the calming talk in the world would never be enough to relax me. I start sweating profusely. I worry that when I leave the chair there is going to be a big puddle of fear left behind.

As I'm in such a state, Mrs Jefferson gives up. She says: "Let's make another appointment and next time I will arrange for some intravenous sedation so that you don't go into shock again."

"Can't you knock me out altogether?"

Mrs Jefferson explains that his would mean a long wait for a hospital operation. She reassures me that the sedation will be more than enough to get me through the process. Then she tells me how much this is all going to cost. I almost start shaking again.

When I get into work at eleven, John comes straight over to my desk.

"You okay, Grace? You look grey."

"I'm fine," I reply. "Had a bit of a bad time at the dentist, that's all."

"Well, as long as you're okay, I won't feel bad about landing you with a heap of work. The advertising team have done a sterling job and we have four extra pages to fill this week. I say 'we', but I mean you. I have non-stop management meetings to go to."

Once John has gone, instead of getting stuck into writing as I should, I check my personal emails. I have replies from everyone I sent out feelers to. First, I read the one from Emma. She asks if I am interested in some freelance work. I am! I quickly reply. Second, I read the one from Michelle in New York. She tells me all about her exciting life she is leading and then at the very end informs me that there is no possible work for me there. Oh well, that would have been too exciting to be true if there had been. Last, I open the email from Peter at *The Yorkshire Mail*. He says there is a vacancy for a features editor, and would I like to apply? My gut reaction is that I don't want to. *The Yorkshire Mail* is a proper, respected newspaper. There is little chance I would get the job, but if I did, would I really like to live in Leeds again? I decide that nothing ventured, nothing gained, and quickly reply yes before I change my mind.

"Good to see you have got typing straight away."

I jump, startled to see John back at my desk. "Oh yes," I lie, "I'm just sending out emails to some of my best sources."

Something about me saying this tickles John, who starts laughing. "Your best sources?" he splutters. "You mean you know more than one old lady with a cat in Dashford?"

"Just you wait, John – when you hear what I have planned, you might want to sit down first, in case you collapse with the thrill of it all."

"Sorry, Grace, I can't face too much excitement right

now – have to get my straight face before I meet the top brass. I could just about squeeze in a coffee first, though. Fancy joining me?"

I decline, as I actually do need to start doing some work, but am much relieved that John is treating me like he used to, as if our embarrassing conversation in the Golden Pineapple a few weeks ago never happened. Does that mean he is no longer interested? I know I should work out how that makes me feel, but luckily I have work to distract me.

I need two good feature ideas for double-page spreads. I hunt through press releases and call my regular contacts. No joy. There are no crimes, no school fetes, no vandalism, and no resident complaints about loud noise. If only there could be a big storm with flooding and trees destroying houses! The weather is being so boring right now – a heat-wave would be good, too ...

There is no option but to beg Iris again to let me write about her and her cat-finding talent. I can fill up the rest of the pages with stories of cats from the cat rescue centre. John may not like cat news, but with so many pages to be filled, he can't afford to be fussy.

I try calling Iris, but there is no reply. I decide I will call in on her on my way home.

I do manage to find one other way to fill a spread. I discover that there was a production of *The Importance of Being Ernest* at Woodlands Comprehensive last week, and the school's head of drama has taken plenty of photos. By the time I have written this up and spoken to the proud mum of the leading actor, Dirk, I'm almost the last person out of the office. The mum went on a lot about the super-talented Dirk, who apparently is destined for great success on the stage. She was pleased she had the foresight to name

him after Dirk Douglas. "Don't you mean Kirk Douglas? Or
Dirk Bogarde?" I asked. "Oh whatever, my Dirk is destined
to be greater than either of them anyway!"

As I tidy up my desk, getting ready to leave, I smell hot
food, something meaty like a sausage roll. I look around and
see that Charlotte is still in the office, sitting at her desk
eating. Looks like a pasty, I decide. She really doesn't look
like the sort of woman who eats pasties; I'm surprised.

I walk past her desk on my way out. "Working late
Charlotte?" I ask.

"Not really, I thought I'd have something to eat here
before I go to my volunteer job."

"That's impressive, doing volunteer work as well as
slaving away for the *Dashford Times*. What do you do?"

"I'm a Samaritan, but I'm not really supposed to talk
about it."

I do my best to stay composed. "That must be really
hard sometimes. Good for you."

I feel my face go bright red and burning hot. I hope
Charlotte hasn't noticed. I mumble goodbye and hurry out
of the building as quickly as possible. As soon as I hit the
high street, I'm in a right state, fearful that amongst all the
calls I have made to the Samaritans over the years I might
have spoken to Charlotte. Surely, though, if Charlotte had
any suspicion she had ever taken a call from me as a Samaritan, she would never have mentioned her volunteer work.
Would she?

It is close to seven pm, so I wonder if it is a little late to
call on Iris. I decide that I need to do something to distract
myself; plus, I genuinely am desperate for a story. As I walk
up the cracked footpath to her front door, I begin to regret
my offer to help with the garden. There is so much that
needs attention, and after the weekend, I'm in no mood to

do any more gardening for a while. Gardens are demanding – no matter how much you do, there is always more to be done.

I knock on the door and soon hear the sound of Iris's footsteps on the hallway tiles. She doesn't open the door, but calls out in a fearful voice, "Who's there?"

"It's me – Grace. I tried to call you to ask if—"

Iris flings open the door. "If I had known you were coming, I would have cooked for you," she says, and she gives me one of her birdlike embraces.

"I don't want to put you to any trouble; I just want to beg you to help me out with a story."

"Come in! Come in! It's such a treat to have you come and visit me again. You will stay for a cup of tea?"

"Yes please, Iris, but I promise not to bother you for too long."

As Iris moves about her 1950s original-décor kitchen, which would be super fashionable if it looked a lot less worn-out, I look at some photographs on the mantelpiece over the lounge fireplace.

One picture, black-and-white, is of a young couple. The woman in the picture could be Iris, when she was in her twenties. She is wearing a smart skirt suit, circa 1940s, with a corsage pinned to her jacket lapel. She is arm in arm with a young man, also smartly dressed in a suit. They are both smiling broadly. It is a grey day, and the stone steps they are standing on are shining as though it has been raining.

Iris walks in with a tray. As a semi-professional biscuit eater, I'm satisfied to see a plate piled high with a variety of classic biscuits.

"Is this you, Iris?" I ask, pointing to the picture.

"Yes, that's on our wedding day." She puts the tray on a

coffee table that has a glass top with a picture underneath of a flamenco dancer in a glorious, frothy, red dress.

"Sit down, dear, and I will tell you about Eric, my husband."

"Only if you want to," I say, "I don't want to pry."

"I like to talk about Eric. As long as you don't go writing about him in the paper of yours!"

This makes me feel a bit guilty, because if this turns out to be interesting, that is exactly what I will want to do.

Iris hands me a cup of tea and offers me the plate of biscuits. I take a bourbon, whilst deciding that I will follow it up with a pink wafer.

"Eric was a kind, gentle man. We were very happy, but he died young. Just two years after that photograph was taken."

"I'm so sorry. What happened?" Phew, too long ago for it to be a local news story.

Iris's blue eyes begin to overflow and she takes a tissue from a ceramic tissue-box holder on the flamenco table. She dabs at her eyes.

"Please don't upset yourself, Iris. We can talk about something else."

"I like to remember him," she sniffs. "Eric worked on the trains, so he'd often take me away at weekends. We liked to get the train down to the south coast and walk and walk. Our last trip was to the Isle of Wight." Iris's voice wobbles and she stops to dab at her tears again.

I move to sit next to her on the sofa and pat her arm.

"Thank you, dear, you are sweet. There was an accident. We were walking along the cliffs between two towns on the east coast – Bembridge and Sandown. We had Snap with us, our collie, when suddenly he took off, chasing a rabbit, probably. Eric doted on that dog. He ran after him.

There was a piercing yelp just after Snap disappeared out of sight towards the edge of the cliff. Eric speeded up, following Snap ..." Iris's sniffles become sobs.

I put my arm around her, careful not to squeeze, as she is such a delicate little thing. I don't say anything and we stay like that for a few minutes.

Rocking slightly as she speaks, Iris continues: "I called out to him to leave Snap, I begged him to come back ..." Iris shakes off my arm and stands up. She walks over to the wedding picture and picks it up. Speaking to it, she says: "What a fool you are, Eric. Killing yourself to save a dog."

I get up and stand next to Iris.

"I don't know what to say."

Iris links her arm with mine and I guide her back to the sofa. We sit quietly for a while.

"It was a terrible time," Iris says. "I lost the only man I ever loved. And the only dog I ever had, too."

"Did you ever think of marrying again?" I ask.

"Oh no, no one could ever take Eric's place."

After what I think is a respectful amount of time, I start drinking my tea again and reach for the pink wafer.

"I do like to see someone who enjoys their food," says Iris. "I have never held with any of that dieting nonsense."

"I'm not surprised. There is nothing of you, Iris, I can't imagine you have ever needed to lose weight."

"I can still get into the same clothes today that I wore on my wedding day," Iris says. "I still have that dress suit upstairs, you know."

As the conversation moves to a less distressing direction, I consider whether it would be acceptable to ask Iris about writing about her and the cats again. As being tactless is one of my fortes, I decide to give it a go.

To my surprise, Iris soon comes around to the idea – as

long as I promise to show her what I am planning to publish so that it isn't a nasty shock. She says she will do it as a favour to me, since I seem to be such a nice, young woman. Seeming to be a nice woman is another one of my fortes. I take a small camera out of my handbag to take her picture.

"Just let me put on something smarter first," says Iris.

"You look fine as you are, and anyway, no one will notice what you're wearing if you are holding a cat."

Iris gets up. "Even so, I'd like to make myself presentable. Help yourself to some more biscuits while you wait."

So I do – a jam cream sandwich and a chocolate covered digestive. When Iris comes back, she is wearing the brown, floral dress she wore when I first came to tea.

"Where shall I sit?" she asks.

"The sofa is fine." I point to a ginger cat asleep on a nearby armchair. "Could you hold the cat?"

"Seems a shame to disturb Cheshire when he's fast asleep," Iris says, "but I'm sure he won't mind this once."

She bends down and quickly up picks the cat, despite the fact that he looks like he is quite a weight, then carries him to the sofa where she sits down with him on her lap, which he overflows as he is a large cat and she is a tiny woman. He carries on sleeping throughout the whole manoeuvre.

"Goodness, what an amenable cat. Neither of my two would put up with treatment like that."

"Cheshire is a lovely old thing," Iris says with a smile.

And I take a picture of Iris grinning, with Cheshire, the cat.

Confession, Part Ten

Often, in the early years, when I was home alone in Conrad's flat, I was happy to plonk myself in front of the TV. In the run-up to the wedding, though, I was so preoccupied and full of plans that I found it hard to focus on any programmes. Instead, I would try to get stuff done. One night, four months before the big day, I decided I needed to finalise the holiday plans. I still wasn't sure where to go – I had got the shortlist down to three places, Barcelona, New York, and Berlin.

As we had already been to New York together, I knew how much Conrad loved the city, but still, I was leaning towards going somewhere Conrad had never been. Somewhere that would be new to both of us. Whenever Conrad planned a trip, he would always research where he was going, so he had a sizeable collection of travel books and guides. I wasn't absolutely sure if Conrad had "done" Berlin or Barcelona already, but I reasoned that if I could find a book on either of those cities, I could cross it off my list. Conrad didn't like to keep all his books on shelves, as he thought that looked like clutter. Instead, he stored most of his books in plastic boxes under the wardrobe and under the bed.

First, I checked under the wardrobe, where there were six boxes neatly labelled. I pulled them all out, thanking him silently when I saw that one was labelled "Travel guides and maps". Bingo. As I lifted up the box, a large manila envelope fell to the ground; it must have been hidden underneath, stored between two boxes. The envelope was not labelled and not sealed. How I wish it had been sealed. Or that I hadn't been so nosey.

I put my hand inside the envelope and pulled out

photographs. The first one I saw was a ten by eight, a group shot of Conrad at his graduation. He was standing in his cap and gown with a group of other students, Charlie at his side. They were all grinning and holding up their beribboned graduation certificates. I flicked through the other pictures, when I realised that perhaps they were private. No perhaps about it – one definitely contained privates. It was a shot of Conrad, naked, reclining on a rumpled bed. He was not looking at the camera, but you could clearly see what sort of mood he was in. I was unnerved by the fact that he had a) allowed someone to take a picture of him like that; and b) kept the photograph. He had always told me that he found pornography and naked pictures a turn-off rather than a turn-on.

I wondered if there would be a companion picture of whoever had taken the shot, but I didn't want to torture myself with seeing images of a past lover. I decided to put the pictures away. As I gathered them together, I couldn't help but glimpse other shots that were clearly pornographic. I didn't examine them, as I had already seen enough naked flesh. Also, they were obviously something that was personal to Conrad – something he wanted to keep hidden. I couldn't help but notice one picture, though, as it slipped out of my hands and skidded away from me. As I hastily retrieved it, I saw enough, more than enough, of someone I recognised.

Instead of admitting to myself what I had seen, and worse, admitting what that meant, I deceived myself. I couldn't bear the ramifications. Plus, there was a small chance there was an innocent explanation. I was never going to confront Conrad with it; I couldn't face his fury about my snooping. Or perhaps I couldn't face finding out the full truth, as it would mean cancelling the wedding.

I distracted myself immediately by opening the box of holiday guides. Here, I found a guidebook to Berlin, but nothing on Barcelona. So that was settled then. We were going to Spain.

By the time I was watching the evening news, with Miro on my lap and Blake at my side, I had completely forgotten that photograph. Except, of course, I never could forget that photograph.

Chapter Twelve

Friday, 26 July 1996

I have taken the afternoon off work as Ruth and I are going
to give the twins a swimming lesson. A private lesson in a
private pool, as Ruth's parents have their own outdoor
swimming pool. Ruth and I used to spend our summer days,
rain or shine, floating about on that pool on lilos, slathered
in body oil if there was even a glimmer of sun, hoping to get
fried a deep, crispy brown. Often, I succeeded in frying
myself and would have nights of agony, where I couldn't

find any sleeping position that didn't put pressure on tender, burnt flesh.

Ruth picks me up, with Horrible and Fighty strapped into car seats in the back. It is about five miles to her childhood home – her parents needed more of a rural setting to fit in such a grand house. When you look over their back fence, you see actual fields. The house is Georgian, with a gravel drive, the sort of thing you often see in TV detective dramas. In fact, you may well have seen it on TV, as it has been used as a location for a fictional crime series where a village, not unlike Dashford, had the misfortune to become the crime capital of the UK, with fresh homicides each week. In reality, there is fewer than one murder every ten years in our town. Lucky for me, so far, I have not been found out.

On the way there, I tell Ruth about my visit to Iris and the story of how her husband died.

"Was anyone else there?" asks Ruth.

"No, that's why they couldn't get help when the dog disappeared."

"Sounds like she knocked off her old man. Literally – knocked him off the cliff edge. She's not just a cat kidnapper; she's a murderer as well." Ruth snorts with laughter as she changes gears, which give out a nasty sounding screech. I'm not sure which sound is more grating: her laugh or the grinding metal.

"Oh, very funny, Ruth. Do you see murderers and criminals in all corners of Dashford?"

"Well, I've got my eye on you, Grace!"

I know Ruth is joking, but I wonder if it ever crosses her mind that I might have been responsible for the death at my wedding. I try to sound light-hearted as I say: "Is that why you keep quizzing me about the wedding? To get me to confess?"

"Absolutely, who knows better than I do what a natural-born criminal you are. You were always pinching Twix fingers out of my lunchbox."

"That was your own fault for not eating them quickly enough. And I was a deprived child – my mother never put any chocolate in my lunch box." This conversation comes to an abrupt end when I screech "Red light!". Just in time, too.

Ruth's parents are away on holiday and have asked us to water the plants. We decide to do this before going swimming, as Fergus and Horace love playing with the hose.

Soon, the twins are running around the garden in their matching swimming shorts decorated with sharks, which I'm not sure is the best motif. Maybe that's because ever since seeing the film *Jaws* I'm always worried I will catch sight of a shark when I go swimming, even in a pool. The boys are soon dripping wet, their blond frizzy mops turning into curls that reach down to their shoulders. Ruth and I also have our swimsuits on, and our towels are spread out on two loungers.

We have brought the boys here several times before to encourage them to start swimming, but they seem to be only interested in ducking each other, making big splashes, and screaming as loud as they possibly can. They are not keen to do anything as boring as swimming.

Ruth realises she has left the twins' inflatable arm bands in the car. She leaves the garden to get them whilst I sit down on a lounger. I would like to stretch out and relax, but I know that if I do that, I will never want to get up. Plus, I have to watch the twins.

Thank God I do.

Fergus is holding the hose and spraying a jet of water

into an arc, whilst Horace runs to and fro underneath, shouting so loudly I wouldn't be surprised if the neighbours call the police to complain about the noise. Even though the next house is about half a mile away. Then, Fergus directs the hose straight at Horace, who screams even louder. I have to put my hands over my ears. Horace runs away towards the pool. I watch him, expecting him to stop at the edge, but he just keeps on running.

There is hardly a splash; instead, there is the shock of sudden silence. I rush to the pool and as I get close, I can see that he is sinking fast, like a stone, with his little arms stretching up and his mouth in a surprised "O" shape. I jump straight in and lift him out.

He coughs and splutters when I sit him on the grass, but he is fine, so I scoop him back up and take him to the lounger where I wrap him in a towel. Fergus runs up to us laughing and then starts chanting: "Horace nearly drowned! Horace nearly drowned!"

Ruth must have heard the chanting as she suddenly appears at the edge of the garden and runs towards us. She starts shouting: "Horace! Did you jump in the water without your arm bands?"

Horace looks up at her angry face and dares not say a word. But Fergus is more than happy to speak for him.

"Horace jumped in the pool. Stupid Horace! I wouldn't jump in the pool without arm bands. I always put arm bands on. Stupid Horace nearly drowned!"

Ruth screams at Horace: "Never, ever do that again! It only takes seconds to drown."

Horace starts crying and I hug him towards me.

"He didn't mean to do it – he was just excited and wasn't watching where he was going. I got him out fast."

Looking drained, Ruth sits down heavily on the other

lounger which promptly collapses, as it isn't built for any weight to land on it suddenly. I try not to laugh, but the boys make no such effort. Soon, Ruth and I are also clutching our stomachs as we become infected with their laughter. The boys start rolling around, still laughing, on the grass.

When we have calmed down, Ruth insists that the boys put on their arm bands immediately. Then she gives me a big hug. I wish I had anticipated this so that I could have prepared myself. I find myself winded and gasping for breath.

"Thank you so much, Grace, you saved my son's life!"

I am speechless, or rather incapable of speech, until Ruth lets me go, and then I feel peculiar. Peculiar in a good way. I'm flooded with relief. I'm not simply a person who pushes people into the water; I'm someone who pulls them out, too. I might not have completely redeemed myself, but surely I have earnt some brownie points with whoever keeps track of my moral copy book?

The swimming lesson takes longer than usual, as Ruth is now on a mission to teach the boys to swim. But her determination does not get results. After an exhausting hour I suggest to Ruth that she should book some swimming lessons at the local public pool and see if a professional teacher can succeed where we have failed.

The twins fall asleep in the car on the way home. When we arrive at Ruth's, we lift them out of the car, into the house, and upstairs to their beds. I am carrying Horace. Despite how much he makes my arms ache, he is now my favourite as I feel partly responsible for his life. I take it really slowly up the carpeted steps. It would be so easy to slip, fall backwards, and then I imagine both Horace and my head cracking on the stone tiles at the bottom of the stairs. If it were my house, I would place pillows at the end of the staircase. Ruth stomps up without fear. I have tried to tell her a few times about her death-trap stairs, but she never takes any notice.

Once the boys are in their beds, she says: "Right, we'll have a good two hours before they are up again. I have something I want to show you."

"I should be getting home," I say. I have a bad feeling about this.

"Stay!" barks Ruth. "Sit down in the lounge and don't move. I'll get wine."

I do as I am told. When Ruth gets back, she passes me a large glass of red and sets hers down on a side table. She goes to the shelves by the TV and picks out a video to put in the player. Turning to me, she announces: "We're going to watch the wedding video."

Ruth sees the expression on my face, but speaks before I get a chance to complain. "Come on, it's time we moved on with your wedding day story, or we could spend years going over it."

"Okay," I say, "let's do this!" I hug myself to give myself some bravado, but actually, I feel much more ready to face this than I would have thought. I could never have contemplated watching this a few months ago.

The video was shot by Graham, but because the day ended in disaster, he didn't get round to editing it or adding a soundtrack. At the start, there are shots of guests at the Register Office standing around. Graham must have then moved to the entrance to wait for me to arrive, as the next thing you see is me walking down the path towards to camera, arm in arm with my mum. The screen almost looks lighter, as I'm radiating so much joy.

Then we see everyone milling around outside after the

ceremony. I'm now arm in arm with Conrad. We're both smiling, and someone throws a few handfuls of confetti over us, which Conrad waves away.

"Anything to add to this?" asks Ruth.

"I feel a bit sick, but no, at this point of the day you can see that nothing out of the ordinary has happened. It looks like a typical wedding."

"It was a lovely wedding. From my perspective, it felt like everyone was having a great time. For you, Grace, I suppose it must have started going wrong when you heard about your mum's illness."

"That was the first low point, but even after that, I was still so happy to have got married."

The film has now moved to Conrad and me climbing into a large, dark car adorned with some white ribbon. We drive off and there are lots of waving arms. That is the end of the Register Office filming. Next, you see Conrad and me standing in front of a gang plank at Kingston Wharf, greeting guests as they arrive. Everything looks rather grey – grey road, grey riverside, grey sky. Some guests get hand-shakes; others get hugs. From me, that is. Conrad always sticks to handshakes. Even for someone as invested in this video as I am, this is frankly tedious viewing.

Then we're inside the boat, and people are holding glasses of champagne. Conrad and I are apart, chatting to different people. The next scene is of the speeches. Conrad and I are sitting next to each other holding hands. You see us laughing together as the best man makes his speech. The best man was Charlie. Charlie was recently married himself to a girl called Camilla, a Sloane Ranger, all pastel shirts with frilly collars ordained with strings of pearls.

When Charlie appears, Ruth looks at me, waiting for me to say something, so I oblige. "I have to admit, as much as I hate Charlie, he did make a brilliant speech. And Mummy was very taken with him. She told me what a nice man he seemed, such a handsome man, too. She said: 'It's so refreshing to see that not all young people are rude, inconsiderate and full of themselves. Not like your awful friend Skye. She is acting appallingly. Why did you invite her again?'"

Ruth says: "Well, your mum was right. Skye was drunk before she even got to the Register Office."

"Yes, she was completely off her head – I wasn't sure what to do about it."

By coincidence, as we talk about her, Skye appears centre screen. She is leaning heavily on Justin, who appears to be holding her upright.

"You don't see Justin anymore, do you?" asks Ruth.

"That's hardly surprising after what he told Skye."

"Perhaps Skye was lying. You know how she liked to make things up."

"Yes, but in that instance, she was telling the truth."

"Perhaps she guessed the truth – you don't know for sure that Justin told her."

I make a "hmm" noise. Justin hasn't been in touch since the funeral. Whether it is because he blames me, or blames himself, or because I bring back memories for him, I don't know or care. I have no interest in ever seeing him again.

After the speeches, the video moves on to showing people dancing. First, you see Conrad and me doing a slow dance. Conrad is holding me against him tight, my head resting on his shoulder. Then a few other couples join in. They look like terrible movers, but maybe they wouldn't look so bad if you could hear the music that was playing.

The film ends.

"Looking at that," Ruth says, "you would never guess how badly the day ended."

"I suppose Graham was no longer in the mood for filming when everyone started crying. He probably didn't think it appropriate to film the police, either."

"Talking of crying," says Ruth, "you seem remarkably composed."

"Hallelujah! You have cured me Ruth!" I raise both my arms. Ruth's frown stops me from continuing being flippant. "No, it's strange. I feel calm. It's as if I'm watching something that had nothing to do with me. Perhaps it will hit me later."

"Well, if it does, don't call me. I need all the sleep I can get at the moment."

"I never call you in the middle of the night, no matter how bad I feel."

Ruth sighs. "True, you never like to put anyone out too much, do you? You don't want to appear to be a bother. Perhaps you should be more demanding, complain when things go wrong. Throw all your toys out the pram. Or one day, you may find that your resentment builds and builds and you end up exploding."

"If I do explode, I'll try not to make a mess on your carpet."

"That's just my point. You can't even explode without considering the effect it will have on other people. You need to express how you feel straight away, without editing it first."

"Believe me, Ruth. I can react in the moment sometimes."

"Like when exactly?"

For the second time today, I wonder if Ruth suspects. Whether she is trying to get me to confess. We hear a thud come from upstairs that signals the boys have woken up. Time for me to leave.

Confession, Part Eleven

It was a shock at the wedding when I heard that Mummy was terminally ill. When I was growing up after Daddy died, I was fearful every time that Mummy got sick that she was going to die, too. She always survived the regular bouts of extreme illnesses she had, so I began to believe that she was invincible.

The extreme illnesses Mummy had were usually minor viruses, such as colds, but they made her suffer terribly. The first sign that she was ill would be at breakfast. When she didn't appear, I knew it was up to me to check on her. Mark was never any help in these circumstances.

I would trudge up the stairs and knock on Mummy's door. Usually there would be a feeble "come in".

Once inside, Mummy would talk to me in a voice full of pain. Not a voice that was too weak to issue commands, though. There would be plenty of those. First, I must open the curtains. Second, I could not go to school, as I was needed as a nurse. Third, I must call the doctor and insist that Mummy got a home visit.

Calling the doctor's surgery was always excruciating. The receptionist would refuse to send the doctor and insist that if Mummy was that ill, she should call an ambulance. Whenever I passed this message on, Mummy would snarl at me for failing to make it clear how sick she was. Then I would be given a list of chores to do. Go to the chemist, make hot drinks, put a wash on, hoover (Mummy said dust gave her asthma), get food, make supper ... Mummy was never too ill to eat supper. "Got to keep my strength up, or who knows if I will make it through?" She made so much fuss over having a minor bug, and yet, when she did get a terminal disease, she didn't want to tell anyone. She didn't want to make it real by talking about it.

One of the things I was looking forward to about going away to university was not having to look after anyone but myself. That didn't quite go to plan. Skye was almost as demanding as Mummy, and sometimes I had to call for emergency ambulances. The first time was just after our exams, before we all left Leeds for good. I don't know what happened to prompt her to take that overdose – she wasn't nursing a broken heart as far as I knew, and she claimed she wasn't bothered about the exams (which was just as well, as she failed to get her degree).

It was early afternoon when I decided I should check on her, as she was usually up by midday. I went into her room and called her name, and she was lying motionless in bed on her back. I went up to her to see that her mouth was wide open and her breathing sounded laboured. I shook her. I shook her harder. No response. I ran downstairs and dialled 999.

She only stayed in hospital one night. When she came back, she acted as if nothing had happened. She refused to talk about it, or why she had tried to kill herself.

Skye was the first to get a job – her lack of degree did not hold her back. She landed her post at Now! Network with the help of a promotional film she had made at college. A smitten lecturer (married, of course) had put together a reel for her. Skye was dazzling on screen: vibrant, flirty, and witty.

I was next to find work. I had applied for reporting jobs all over the country, but Dashford was the only town that wanted me. As Conrad pointed out, even the *Dashford Times* wasn't that keen to have me; it was just desperate.

Six months later, Justin found work in London as a trainee copywriter at an agency in Baker Street. He is still there, as far as I know.

Justin loved Skye probably more than anyone else has. Her mother was plain negligent judging from the stories Skye told about her childhood, and she never went back home to the commune much, so there can't have been anyone else there she was attached to. I think one reason that Justin adored Skye was because she was so much fun. She was never as demanding of him as she was of me. Justin loved partying with Skye and liked to show her off to his other friends. He adored the celebrity scene, and just like Skye, used to claim to have slept with the most unlikely film and music stars. Whenever I watched TV with him, he would point out different men on screen and say: "He's gay. He's gay. Oh, and he's gay, too."

"They can't all be gay," I would reply when I got fed up with his constant interruptions.

"Well, I know for a fact that *he's* gay, because I slept with him," was the standard response.

After we left Leeds, I found Skye unconscious twice more, both times at my flat. It was strange how she always timed her suicide attempts for when I was due to see her. She always trusted me to save her.

Chapter Thirteen

SMILES COULD SOON BECOME FROWNS

By Grace O'Neill

Over one-third (34 per cent) of borough residents are not registered with a dentist, either private or registered with the

Saturday, 27 July 1996

Today I wake up with a heavy feeling. Not just because it is a Saturday, but because Blake is lying on my chest. He stares at me crossly, his eyes saying: *Get up and feed me! Feed me!*

I'm not looking forward to today, as this morning I'm scheduled to have my tooth out. I have been instructed that I need to be driven home because of the sedation. I don't want to put anyone to any bother at the weekend, so I have booked a taxi to take me there and collect me.

When I'm sitting in the dentist's chair, I feel so scared, I consider getting up and refusing to go through with it. Mrs Jefferson introduces me to the anaesthetist who is administering the intravenous sedation. He is so good looking it is ridiculous – an archetypical dark-haired Adonis. And about my age. This inspires me to be a little braver. Plus Tess, the dental assistant, is a friend of Ruth's, so it would soon get back to Ruth if I was a complete wuss.

Then the drugs get to work and I no longer feel terror. Quite the reverse. I feel brilliant. This is wonderful – I am filled with euphoria. Who could have known that having a tooth out could be such fun?

By one o'clock I am back home, decidedly groggy. I'm lounging in front of the TV and contemplating whether to put a film on, when the doorbell goes. Standing on the doorstep is John, almost hidden behind a bouquet of pink and red flowers, including giant peonies, which are my favourite.

"John! Are those for me? How gorgeous! Come in."

"I just wanted to drop them off; I don't want to disturb you."

"Oh, come in and entertain me. I don't know what to do with myself – I'm lying around being useless."

John has never been inside my house before; I feel self-conscious about how old-fashioned it is. It hasn't been redecorated for at least ten years.

The lounge is painted magnolia-white. There used to be religious pictures hanging on the walls until I removed them after Mummy died. I left one small wooden crucifix up by the front window, as I felt Mummy might come down (or rise up, depending on where she is) and smite me if I removed all traces of God from the house.

"Would you like a tea or coffee?"

"If you're sure it isn't too much trouble ..." says John. "Would you like me to make it? You must be feeling wobbly."

I reassure John that I am fine and give him the good news that I have some of Ruth's home-baked choc-chip cookies in the biscuit tin. I leave John for a few moments whilst I make the drinks and he settles himself down on one of the sagging armchairs. He makes a loud "aaah" sound as he sits down, as if he is exhausted. He has probably been playing rugby or something, followed by a shower, as he looks well scrubbed. What am I doing thinking about John having a shower? Those dentist drugs have done funny things to me.

When I come back and pass him a plate with a cookie on it, John says: "This looks great. We should ask Ruth to write a baking column for the paper."

"She hasn't got the time. Plus, the paper hasn't got the money to pay a decent rate for it. I don't want to start exploiting my friends."

"You were happy enough to exploit that old cat lady," John reminds me. "I have to admit, that piece worked out well. I'm sorry I was so discouraging about it. I should know by now that people love cats."

As if on cue, Blake jumps up and settles on John's lap. John surprises me by going bananas stroking him and cooing at him. I have never seen him like this with Ruth's cat, but then Boris is not such a great cat.

John's coos are in an embarrassing high-pitched tone as he strokes Blake under the chin: "Ooh, you are a gorgeous girl!"

"It's a boy cat, called Blake."

"Hello, Mister Handsome," John whispers, almost seductively.

This is getting awkward.

"I didn't know you liked cats, John. You should get one."

"I have thought about it, but who would look after it when I go away? Too much responsibility. I don't know where I will be in a year's time – not here, that's for sure."

I don't know why I'm so shocked to hear this. Especially as I'm thinking of moving away myself. Did I imagine John would stay in Dashford forever?

"Are you thinking of going because things look a little shaky at the *Times*," I ask, "or have you just had enough of Dashford."

"Even though there will be some cuts at the paper, I think my job is safe – yours too, probably."

"Hurrah!" I say rather flatly, wondering whether I should tell John that I also plan to leave soon. Whether I should mention my interview at *The Yorkshire Mail*.

John continues: "The shake-up at the paper got me thinking that it was about time for me to move on. I should try and do something more challenging before I die. Besides, there is nothing to keep me here anymore."

I ask the obvious: "Anymore?"

John gives me a long look, sighs, puts down his mug and says: "You know very well what I mean. Sorry, Grace, I'd better be off. Thanks for the tea."

I don't stop John from leaving, even though I really want to. The look on his face when he says goodbye makes me feel quite peculiar. I feel like reaching out and grabbing him, but is this because I really want to, or because I think he wants me to? I'm completely confused and those dentist drugs aren't helping me to think clearly at all.

I don't have long to analyse my feelings before I have another visitor. Ruth arrives, with Fighty and Horrible in tow. She shoves them out into the back garden with a football. I don't like to mention that they might destroy all the hard work I have done out there, as I owe Ruth so much. My life, probably.

"I thought I'd better check up on you," she says as she heaves herself down into the armchair John recently vacated. "Have you got any of my cookies left?"

"Just a couple. John was here earlier tucking into them. I'll go and make some tea."

As I go towards the kitchen, Ruth notices the flowers on the coffee table. She touches the leaves. "What gorgeous flowers. Did John bring them? Poor man, he really is besotted."

"Don't say that – it makes me feel ... well ... I don't know what it makes me feel."

"By the time you work it out, it will be too late. I'll tell you how you feel. You like John just as much as he likes you. Why don't you hurry up and do something about it?"

I disappear into the kitchen without saying anything. I busy myself making more hot drinks. I decide I will ignore what Ruth has just said. It is too much to process right now.

When I come back, I'm glad when Ruth changes the subject and asks how the dentist appointment went.

"I tell you, Ruth, the drugs they gave me were beyond fabulous. And the man who gave them to me was the most handsome man I have ever seen off-screen. I wish I could have taken a picture of him to show you. Just imagine the love child of Elizabeth Taylor and Rock Hudson.

"I was transported, by the drugs mainly. Do you remember that day we took acid? Skye gave me some and I was going to get rid of it, but you persuaded me to give it a go with you. We have that wonderful, crazy, afternoon in the park ..."

That's when I have a sudden flashback. Ruth doesn't notice that I have stopped talking mid-sentence, as she is laughing. Eventually, through her giggles, she says: "One of the best days of my life! Never tell Graham about it, you know how he is about drugs."

Rather than respond with something appropriate, I'm saying "Shit, shit, shit" under my breath.

"What on earth is wrong, Grace?"

"I have just remembered something. That stuff they pumped into me at the dentist must have been like a truth drug. I have a distinct memory of telling Mrs Jefferson and Mr Handsome all about me taking acid."

Ruth laughs, and really hard this time. "Oh, that's so funny. I will never be able to look Mrs Jefferson in the eye again. If you told them that, Grace, what else do you think you told them? You must have revealed all your darkest, deepest secrets."

I do not join in the laughter.

"Oh, come on, Grace! Lighten up!"

I sit forwards and put my head between my knees. When I sit back upright, I say: "I'm sorry, Ruth, but I feel sick – must be another reaction to the drugs. I think I'll have to go to bed."

Ruth gets up. "Off you go then, I'll see myself out."

Once she has gone, dragging her muddy boys through my house first, I collapse upstairs in my room.

What am I going to do? I might have told the dentist, the anaesthetist and dental assistant Tess everything. Also there is Charlotte at the office. I might have told her too when she was doing a shift at the Samaritans. Why am I stupid enough to always give my name when I call the

Samaritans? She is bound to have put two and two together. I may as well stick my confession up on a great, big poster and paste it up in the centre of town.

I spend the rest of the day in bed, wondering what will happen when someone contacts the police and tells them what I have done.

Confession, Part Twelve

When Mummy begged me to kill her, how could I say no? She had trained me so well to do what I was told.

I remember every bit of that awful conversation on my wedding day. It took place after the speeches and my first dance with Conrad. As soon as the dancefloor filled up, I stopped dancing and went up to Mummy, who was sitting on her own, looking furious as she had done all day. I sat down next to her.

"Mummy, can we talk?"

"How can we with all this noise?"

That's when I made the mistake of saying "Let's go outside".

Begrudgingly, she came out with me to the small deck at the back of the boat.

"It's chilly out here," she grumbled.

I got straight to the point: "Auntie Maggie has told me."

Mummy walked over to the boat rail. Standing with her back to me, she said: "I told her not to tell anyone. That sister of mine has a mouth on her that can't bear to be shut. Ever since we were wee bairns I have had to put up with a stream of nonsense that that woman speaks ..."

I moved next to her and tried to put my arms around her shoulder, but she was having none of it and pushed me away.

"Just because I am dying, you don't have to start hugging me. Soon I will be in the arms of our Lord; His arms are the only ones that can comfort me now."

"Auntie Maggie said that you don't have long."

"I have too long. That's what I can't stand – all this waiting to die. I don't want to lose all my faculties, control of my body. Have the indignity of other people washing me. I can't let someone else wipe ..." Mummy leant over the rail of the boat as far as she could. "If it weren't a sin, I'd jump off right here, right now."

"Don't be scared about how your illness will affect you. I will be around to make sure you always have your dignity."

Mummy swung around to look at me, her expression fierce. Her cheek was going mental, her eyes wide, and her lips narrowed to a thin line.

"Help me now, Grace," she said.

"Of course I will. I will help you any way I can."

Mummy walked over to a gap in the handrail where two chains took the place of railings. These chains had been temporarily unattached to let us all into the boat. Mummy unhooked them again.

"What are you doing? Stop that, Mummy, it's dangerous!"

"Push me off, Grace. Kill me now. I don't want a lingering death; just push me off and I can sink to a peaceful end now. Kill me, Grace."

She had her back to the water and each arm was extended, holding onto the rails each side of the gap. She swayed back.

"Grace!" she ordered. "Quick, do it now, please. Don't let me fall or I will be committing a sin. Just a small push!"

It would have been far harder to pull her back onto the

boat than push her off the way she was leaning backwards. If I had tried to pull her back, I would surely have been pulled into the water with her. I didn't have much choice, and it was hard to think straight with Mummy constantly repeating: "Push me, Grace, please push me. Push me now!"

Chapter Fourteen

GREENHOUSE RAIDED BY DRUGS PREVENTION SQUAD

By Grace O'Neill

Following complaints that a greenhouse on the Verity
Road Estate allotment contained six-foot-high cannabis
plants, a police unit was deployed to the area and

Sunday, 28 July 1996

I am supposed to be helping Iris out with her garden today,
but I'm shattered. I hardly slept last night and now I lie in a
crumpled heap on the settee, where I have been ever since I
got up to feed the cats.

It is the small, quavering sound of the doorbell that gets
me up. Ruth stands on the doorstep. "Why are you still in
your pyjamas?" she demands. "Have you forgotten our
run?"

"Sorry." I pull a pantomime sad face, damn; I have completely forgotten about this run. I try to make an excuse: "I'm just not up for it today. I'm still feeling feeble from yesterday."

Ruth isn't having any of it. "No excuses. Get your running shorts right now. I'm not running on my own."

Ten minutes later, Ruth is telling me off again as we jog down the street.

"What's wrong with you? At last I thought the old Grace was coming back to me, but you're acting like a zombie again. Why?"

"No reason."

"Don't mess me around, Grace. Something, or some news, has done this to you. What is it?"

"I wish I could tell you, but it wouldn't be fair on you."

Ruth comes to an abrupt halt. I stop, too.

"Okay, now you *have* to tell me. You can't just say that and not tell me. You know the rule."

The rule is that we're not allowed to keep secrets from each other. We swore we wouldn't at a special ceremony in Ruth's bedroom when we were twelve. We dressed up in ceremonial robes (bedspreads), sprinkled salt, lit candles and everything.

"Yes, I know the rule."

"So tell me."

"I can't tell you today because I have to help Iris with her garden."

I can't see Ruth's face because she is now running slightly ahead of me, but I can imagine the fury that is written upon it. I can tell by the way she is running that she is full of anger. The whole pavement shakes every time one of her feet lands and I wouldn't be surprised to see new cracks appear in the paving slabs. I make an effort to get some speed up to catch up with her.

"No matter how late you finish at Iris's," she pants. "no matter how tired you are, you have to tell me everything this evening. Text me when you get home and I'll come straight over."

I promise that I will. By this evening I will have been able to think up a story to fob her off with.

Ruth says: "Don't even consider trying to make something up. I can always tell when you're lying."

Ruth is not alone in thinking she can read me like a book. But truth be told, ironically, I have got away with telling Ruth quite a few fibs over the years.

When I turn up at Iris's house just in the early afternoon, I try to appear normal. It is a perfect day for doing the garden – grey but not raining – so we don't need hats or sunscreen.

Iris opens the door wearing a big man's plaid shirt and some dark nylon trousers. Slacks. Only people her age wear slacks. She gives me her customary fluttery hug and we kiss each other on the cheek. Her cheek feels like the skin you get on cold tea and she smells of baby powder. As she bustles me through the kitchen, I spy a chocolate cake on the kitchen counter. The cake is home-made. I can tell by the indecent amount of butter icing it has and the Smarties decorating it.

"That's your reward for helping me. First of all, it would be wonderful if you could give me a hand pruning a few shrubs. I have plenty of green bags to put the cuttings in. If we could fill three bags and then you take them away with you, I would be so grateful."

"With that cake as an incentive," I reply, "I should be finished in no time."

I follow Iris to the back of the garden, where bushes have taken over to the extent that nothing has been able to grow under them for a long time. Where once there must have been grass, there is brown, dry dirt and dead leaves.

It feels therapeutic chopping away. In my head, I say "Take that, and that and that!" as I cut into them. I'm not angry with anyone else; I'm furious with myself. Furious for having got myself into such a mess.

Iris is working nearer the house. Whereas I'm wielding hefty garden shears, Iris is snipping away with neat little pruning scissors. Yet the piles of leaves and branches at her feet don't seem that much smaller than the piles surrounding me.

Just two hours later, I'm surprised at the dramatic effect we have had on the garden. It already looks much bigger. I start gathering up the cuttings.

Iris tries to help me, but I motion her away. "It's okay, I've got this. You put the kettle on; I can't wait to try that cake."

Soon, the bags of garden waste are in the back of my car, and Iris and I are sitting in her conservatory. Cups of tea and slices of cake are in front of us. My slice is huge, whilst Iris's looks tiny.

As Iris takes a delicate mouthful of cake, I tell her how pleased the editor of the paper was with the story about her and the cats.

"I see you also used a nice picture of Miro in the article," Iris says. "Such a splendid-looking cat."

"Cheshire and you looked good, too. I have something I have been meaning to ask you. When you find the cats, how do you get them home? It is impossible to carry a wriggling cat."

"Wait here," says Iris, and she disappears back into the

main part of the house. A minute later she reappears with a shopping trolley. A bright, orange shopping trolley with white spots.

"I put them in here," she says. "Then it's no trouble transporting them."

An orange shopping trolley with white spots. I remember the bus driver telling me that the woman who *might* have pushed the cyclist over had a trolley like this. And she also had long dark hair, just like Iris has.

"Where did you get such a bright trolley?" I ask to give myself time to process my thoughts before I start throwing around accusations. "It certainly stands out."

"Yes, doesn't it," Iris says, beaming. "You won't see anyone else around here with one like this. I didn't want a boring, drab trolley like everyone else has, like I used to have, in fact. I saw this when I went on a cross-Chanel shopping trip, and I couldn't resist it."

"This may seem like a strange question, but were you on the bridge one rainy morning a few weeks ago? When there was that bike accident?"

A second ago Iris looked all inflated with pride. Now she looks as if someone has removed her stopper. She deflates in front of me, crumpling into her chair. She puts her elbows on the table and her head in her hands. Starts weeping, silently.

I put out my arm to pat at one of Iris's heaving shoulders.

"Oh, Iris," I say, "it was you the bus driver saw, wasn't it? She said she saw you on the bridge at the time, right next to the man on the bike before he fell."

Iris says nothing and keeps her head down.

"It must have been a huge shock for you," I add.

I feel like sobbing myself. I can imagine how

distraught Iris must have felt seeing the accident. I remember how I felt after ... Iris brings me back to her tragedy, rather than mine, by saying in a small voice: "It was awful. What is truly terrible is that I sometimes think it was my fault. I could be partly to blame for that poor, poor man's death."

I don't say anything, but continue patting ineffectually at Iris's shoulder. Iris is silent for a good few beats before she speaks again.

"I didn't mean to do it. It all happened so quickly and I am not sure exactly of the details. He must have been going ever so fast – he was far too close to the pavement. I felt him brush against me. It gave me a fright. That's when I might have done a terrible thing, though I'm not sure if I am imagining it because of the shock. I think I might have reacted in a terrible way."

Trying to keep my voice steady, I ask: "In what way?"

"As I say, I can't be sure. I torture myself that I must have put my arm out, because I thought I was going to fall, but instead of steadying myself, I might have ended up shoving the man on the bike. Oh, I wish I could remember for sure! I know that I felt him brush against me. I know I lost my balance a little and the next thing he was in the road. I couldn't bear to look because I could hear the bus brakes and then a nasty, nasty metal sound. There was no way I could turn my head to see. I could not bear to see. So I just kept on walking. On and on."

Iris starts crying again.

"Hush, Iris. The man probably lost his balance because he hit the kerb. He was probably trying to swerve away from you when he touched you and lost control."

Iris looks up, her tear-stained face full of hope. "Do you think so, dear? Do you really, really think so?"

"Well, you would never have deliberately pushed him, would you?"

"No, no, no, of course I wouldn't. It's not just that, though. I should have gone to the police. I tried to forget about the whole thing instead. Forget it ever happened, but I keep remembering. A few days afterwards, the bus driver saw me as I was walking over the bridge and stopped her bus to jump out and talk to me. I thought she was going to accuse me of murder, but all she did was tell me to go to the police. I hoped that if I didn't do anything and tried not to think about it, eventually it would go away. It has never gone away."

"I can imagine," I say. I know exactly how she feels. I then give Iris the advice that I know I should follow myself: "You can still go to the police. It will help to put your mind at rest. There is no way you will be charged with anything, I'm sure the police will take a statement and that will be it. From what you've said, it was a clearly an accident."

"Then you will write about it in that paper of yours and everyone will be talking about it. About me!"

I didn't respond immediately, as I needed to give this some thought. John was sure to find out from the police if Iris went in to give a witness statement. He would then put pressure on me to write a follow-on story. I couldn't see how this could be avoided.

"Maybe there is another way to put this behind you. You have told me now, so at least you don't have to keep this to yourself any more. See how you feel in a few days' time. If it hasn't helped telling me, then I would seriously consider going to the police. Perhaps I can persuade my editor not to publish anything."

Slowly, Iris gets back her composure, though she never touches her cake. She urges me to finish my slice, which I do, out of politeness. It is like eating sand, my mouth feels so dry. This whole scene with Iris has resurrected a lot of bad feelings.

Iris, on the other hand, seems completely recovered. She says: "I must thank you, not just for doing my garden, but for listening to me. You don't know how much better you make me feel, Grace. You are a ray of sunshine. The world is a brighter place for having you in it."

An emptier place, I think.

"Thanks for the cake," I mumble as I get up to leave. Iris has given me the remaining cake in an old Quality Street tin. "I will drop off this tin soon, the minute I get back from a trip to Leeds I'm taking next week."

"I didn't know you were going up north?"

"Yes, I have an interview up there. Plus, I went to university in Leeds, so I want to spend some time visiting my old haunts."

As I walk away, I turn to see Iris waving at me. "Have a great trip! And don't worry about that old tin – I have plenty of them."

On the way home I drop off the bags of garden waste at the council dump. As I drive, I start to shake, which makes it hard to keep control of the clutch. I decide that I will need to take some tranquilisers when I get back into my house. Which is exactly what I do.

Two Diazepam and a hot shower later, I'm sitting in my lounge feeling as though I'm waiting for an executioner, as Ruth is due any minute. I'm wearing pyjamas – I plan to go to bed the minute Ruth leaves.

When Ruth arrives, I offer her coffee and a piece of Iris's cake.

"You certainly have a knack for getting people to bake

for you. Now that you have Iris meeting your sweet-tooth needs, maybe I can give up feeding you."

"Don't you dare. I live for your fudge, cakes, and cookies. Life would be empty without them."

"Your stomach would be emptier, at least. Talking of which, I have noticed my waistbands are getting a bit looser – are yours?"

"I can't say I've noticed."

Ruth appraises me. "I reckon you're looking a bit slimmer, not that you needed to lose weight. It must be all the running we're doing."

"Plus I have been gardening," I add. "My arms ache like mad right now."

Ruth settles herself down on the settee and pats the space next to her for me sit there.

"That's enough small talk. No more prevaricating. Tell me your deep, dark secret."

I sit down. I put my hands face up in my lap and stare down at my palms.

"Stop admiring your green fingers and tell me everything," orders Ruth.

Thanks to Iris, I don't have to think too hard about what to say.

"It was silly that I got into such a state when we were on our run earlier. It's just that I realised that I might have told the dentist a secret. A secret I promised not to tell anyone."

"So it's not your secret, then? It's someone else's?" Oh good, looks like I might be able to get away with this.

"Yes, that's why I can't tell you. You wouldn't want me to spill the beans about you to anyone else, would you?"

"No, of course not, but I am a special case. You *have* to keep my secrets. You also have to never keep secrets from me. That's what we agreed."

"We agreed that when we were kids, though!"

"Oh for heaven's sake, you know you have to tell me. Stop taking your time over it and spit it out."

Ruth grabs a cushion which she hugs and settles back further into the settee.

"Why do you always hug cushions?" I ask.

"You often hug cushions, too – it's reassuring. Don't try to change the subject; just tell me the secret."

So I explain how Iris thinks she might have accidentally knocked the cyclist who died under the bus. After I finish, Ruth stares at me wide eyed. Then her eyes narrow and a frown appears.

"That is not the secret that is eating away at you. I have a great deal I would like to say about what you have just told me – such as how it proves that Iris is a woman with a dark, dark, nature. You should stay away from her. Right now, however, we need to get to the truth. I know what is upsetting you is to do with your wedding day. I know in my bones that you have got yourself into a state imagining somehow that you're to blame for everything that happened that day. I just know you have been rewriting history. I understand you so well."

Ruth's voice remains level as she continues: "Don't you remember how for days afterwards, no, for weeks afterwards, we would talk about what happened again and again. We talked about it until we had it straight in our heads. Tell me what you now think happened, so I can tell you the truth about that day. So you can believe it once and for all!"

"Leave it, Ruth, just leave it!" I shout. "You don't know me as well as you think! And you don't know Iris either. She is not some evil witch like you make out. If anyone is an evil witch, it is—"

Ruth holds up her hand and it is her turn to shout. "Stop there!" She stands up abruptly. "That is it, I'm done. I'm no longer going to support you living in a dream world. When you're ready to confront the truth, I'm happy to help you. Don't bother calling me ever again until we can have an honest conversation."

I don't know what to say; I don't have much time to say anything anyway. Ruth is soon at my front door and then she is soon on the other side of it, having slammed it loudly shut.

"Shit!" I say after she has left. Not just because I'm upset about what she has said, but because I worry who is going to feed my cats when I'm away for two nights next week now that Ruth is out of my life?

Confession, Part Thirteen

At first, after Ruth left, I didn't know what to do with myself. I thought about calling the Samaritans again, but with Charlotte working there, I didn't dare. Since that evening when I found out she was a Samaritan, I'm sure I have caught her giving me strange looks.

I also torture myself with the thought that I might have told Tess, Ruth's friend, about the murder when I was under sedation. The net is closing in. I now think Ruth knows the truth, too, but wants to convince me that my memory is at fault, rather than admit that I am.

One of my tactics when I feel like this is to message Mark. So I do. I just write: *"How are you?"*

I'm not surprised when Mark ignores the question and messages straight back: *"Okay, what is wrong?"*

"Mark, I can't keep it in anymore. I have to confess. I am a murderer."

"*What are you talking about? Are you having crazy thoughts about your wedding day again?*"

"*It's not just that. You know I killed Mummy. You were there.*"

Mark's next text reads: "*Yes, I was there. So I know you didn't kill her. Her death wasn't anyone's fault. You always do this. Blame yourself for everything.*"

I stop texting. This isn't really helping. Mark always says what I want him to.

Chapter Fifteen

**NEW FLIGHT PATH CAUSES
POLLUTION CONCERNS**

By Grace O'Neill

A local residents committee, keen to fight a proposed flight-path
proposal, has put together a list of possible noise and air pollution

Thursday, 1 August 1996

I have to get up at six am to get my train into London where
I will then pick up the train to Leeds. I leave out plenty of
cat food for Miro and Blake to last them today. I have
arranged for my neighbour to pop in and feed them
tomorrow and Saturday morning. I was very embarrassed to
have to ask Mr Harrison next door, as we aren't on the best
of terms. Even though he has lived next door (all alone) for
as long as I can remember, he has never let me call him

anything but Mr Harrison. The only times I have spoken to him recently have been when he has come round to complain about Miro and Blake messing in his back garden, as if there is something I can do about it.

I went over last night with a nice bottle of wine and was as ingratiating as I could be. There was simply no one else I could think of asking to feed the cats, as John is away at the end of this week, too. I just hope that by getting to know the cats a bit better, Mr Harrison will feel more kindly towards them. And not put something horrid in their food ...

On the train to Leeds, I do some research into latest goings-on in Yorkshire, prepping for my interview which is this afternoon. As I read articles from *The Yorkshire Mail* I worry that I'm not up to the job – seems there is a lot more going on around Leeds, and the features are far more in-depth and analytical than I'm used to. There is also a lot more sport: the cricket team features heavily. I know hardly anything about sport. I am doomed to embarrass myself. I wish I could turn around right now.

I close my laptop for a break and find my thoughts keep returning to Mummy and her death. When she asked me to push her off the boat at the wedding, I almost reached out my hand to do as she asked. Almost. Instead, I turned around and walked away. I heard no splash, no scream. I knew she would not allow herself to fall in the river, and she didn't.

It was two months later that she died. I moved into her house soon after my wedding, so at least I spent the last few months of her life caring for her as best I could. I blame myself for how Mummy's life ended because I didn't try to persuade her to have treatment, treatment that could have prolonged her existence for maybe up to another year. I was a terrible daughter. Her last words to me were: "I hope you don't feel guilty when I am dead."

"Why should I feel guilty?" I asked.

"Well, if you don't have a conscience ..." Her voice was weak and her grip on my hand even weaker. I held on to it until the last.

Now I do feel guilty, so at least that means I must have some sort of conscience. One redeeming feature.

My mobile rings, and I get a cross look from the man sitting opposite me as I answer. Even though he has been on the phone himself for at least half of the journey so far. I suppose he feels his calls were important, as he looks like he has some big job – he is wearing a very smart suit.

It is John on the phone. "Where are you?" he asks, though I told him I was going away for a few days. But I didn't mention the interview.

"You know I would be away."

"Yes, though you never told me where you were going, I just wondered if you can speak now or you are on a train or something, in case we get cut off. I have some rather big news."

"Actually, I am on a train."

"Okay, well I will keep it short, and if we get cut off, I will send you a text. But here are the headlines. Your friend Iris has been arrested. She was caught trying to grab a pedigree Persian cat from Marjorie the Mayor of Dashford's back garden. She is now under investigation for catnapping local cats. Ruth has already been questioned this morning and the police want to talk to you. I have told them you're away, so they want you to go into the station and give a statement as soon as you're back."

I'm obviously stunned. I don't speak.

"You still there, Grace?"

"Yes, I'm lost for words."

"Where are you going, by the way? And when are you back?"

"I'm going back to my old stomping ground from uni days, Leeds."

I hear John gasp, as if I have given him some momentous news. Soon I find out I have.

"I don't believe it! I'm coming up to Leeds tomorrow!"

"Why on earth?"

"Let's meet up tomorrow evening, if you're free, and I can tell you why."

I agree to text John a suggestion for a time and place to meet for dinner tomorrow. As soon as the call is over, I am even less composed than I was before. So much for getting away from everyone for a few days. How am I possibly going to be able to do a decent interview when my mind is all over the place?

Yet, surprisingly, I am rather brilliant in the interview, even if I say so myself. To prove I am not exaggerating how well it went, I am offered the job of features editor on the spot. No nepotism involved, as my old colleague Peter isn't in the interview; I am interviewed by the editor, a woman called Jane Whitman, who obviously took a liking to me. We quickly found out that we share a love of cats, chocolate, and *Coronation Street*, so we bonded instantly.

Unlike my job at the *Dashford Times*, I'm not offered the position because I am the only person interviewed, as five others have gone before me. Apparently, none of them had my portfolio of past features, or seemed to have such enthusiasm for the paper and such knowledge of Yorkshire. Luckily, I was not expected to know anything about sport, as this is an area I will never be covering. Result! Or is it, I wonder once I'm alone in my hotel room.

The hotel is a Hilton, but I got the room at a bargain rate. I asked for a single, but there are two double beds in the room, which is spacious, clean, and has a gleaming bathroom full of mini toiletries that I plan to steal.

I said at the interview that I was very excited about the job and that as soon as I got my official offer, I would call Jane to confirm when I could start. But do I really want to live in Leeds again? I don't know many people here. There are a few people from uni who still live in Leeds, but I haven't seen or heard from them in years. They weren't good enough friends to invite to my wedding.

But being away from Dashford has somehow made me feel lighter. Moving away from where I have made so many bad decisions, done so many bad things, may be the best way forwards.

I decide to sleep on it and spend all of tomorrow walking around the area and seeing if I can really imagine myself living here again.

Deciding to sleep on it, unfortunately, does not help me to get to sleep.

At first, my mind is full of how my new life could be and all the logistics of moving here. Renting out my house, finding somewhere here to live, proving myself in a new job … It will all be stressful. Then I remember John's phone call whilst I was on the train. I sit bolt upright. Iris has been arrested! How can I dream of making a new life, when chances are I'm going to be the next woman arrested in Dashford? And for murder. The only life I will be having is one in prison.

To stop myself imagining the drama of being found guilty of murder, followed by incarceration, I decide maybe I should message Mark again. Although, being in Leeds, that somehow seems a ridiculous thing to do. In this hotel bedroom so far away from home, I'm less able to convince myself that Mark is still alive. What is the point of making up texts from him; what is the point of pretending he is looking out for me still? At least his death is one I cannot possibly be blamed for, even though, deep down, I have always felt it was somehow my fault.

Confession, Part Fourteen

I never met Mark, the living, breathing Mark; I have only lived with his ghost all my life. I have seen him grow up, as clearly as I have seen my own reflection in the mirror, but only in my imagination. He died six months after he was born. Mummy went to wake him up from his afternoon nap, but there was no waking him. "He looked so perfect when I found him," Mummy used to say. "There was no illness. God must have wanted him by his side, because he was such a lovely baby." I was born on Mark's actual birthday, when he would have been two years old.

It was Mummy who brought Mark to life for me, who made out he was living with us still. She spoke of him all the time; she kept the bedroom that would have been his spotless. It was decorated all in blue, from the curtains to the sheets on the small, single bed. She celebrated every one of his birthdays by baking a special chocolate sponge cake for him, which was always bigger than the vanilla sponge cake she would bake me ("There's no way we can eat two big cakes!" she would say). She would insist I blow out all the candles on both cakes. When I blew out the candles on Mark's cake she would close her eyes tight whilst she made a wish. When I asked her what she was wishing for, she would always say that it was a wish that could never come true. She wished that Mark was still alive. She may not have added the words *Instead of you*, because that didn't need to be said.

Mummy made it clear in so many little ways how much better it would have been for her if Mark had stayed alive and she hadn't had to have another child. She would say she could never have managed two children – that would have been far too much work. The way she looked at me on my birthday, on our birthdays, spoke of her deep sadness that it was me blowing out candles, not Mark. No wonder I felt guilty.

To make her feel better, I used to tell her that I saw Mark, that he was a proper big brother to me. Teasing me sometimes, playing with me others, protecting me always. Mummy used to look so happy when I said I had been out with Mark in the garden, or I used to lay an extra place for him at the tea table. I didn't feel I was making it up, it felt so real. I could see him and hear him. I have distinct memories of being with him.

Ruth used to indulge me and pretend when she came over that she could see Mark too. "Mark is so much fun!" she would sometimes say. When we'd play board games, the three of us, it must have been Ruth who threw the dice for Mark's turn. It was surprising how often he won – he was particularly good at Monopoly.

When we became teenagers, Ruth got tired of joining in my fantasy that Mark was still alive. When I spoke about seeing him, she didn't tell me that I was mad to have an imaginary big brother. She would just roll her eyes. She still does. I don't know why she lets me talk about him so much – perhaps it is because she is a good friend and she knows what a comfort Mark is to me.

Or rather, she was a good friend. I have even messed up that relationship now.

Chapter Sixteen

HEARSE GETS PARKING TICKET IN HIGH STREET

By Grace O'Neill

Immediately following a funeral last Wednesday, 31 July, a hearse from the funeral company of Wake and daughters was given

Friday, 2 August 1996

After no sleep whatsoever, I give up and get up just before six am. I open the curtains to see the city beginning to wake up below me. I am high up, on the tenth floor, so the view is good, even though it is of central Leeds, so not very green. I can see tops of buildings and quiet roads, with just a few vans making deliveries. Everything is shining, as it must have been raining and the sun's rays bounce off windows and buildings. The city has never looked so beautiful to me.

I put on some leggings and trainers and head out for a run. The streets are quiet, so I don't have to avoid anyone as I run along the pavements, all around the main sites of the city, past the many shopping centres and the city's art gallery.

As I run, I come to a decision. I cannot wait for my crime to catch up with me. I will go to the police when I get back to Dashford and confess everything. I have been punishing myself so much over the last two years, prison can't be any worse. Right now, I must live right for the moment and make the most of my last days of freedom, do everything that will bring me joy.

I spend the rest of the day doing exactly that. I have a full English breakfast at the hotel, followed by a visit to the city gallery. I buy a sandwich and chocolate to have in my room, and spend the rest of the day watching TV from my bed. I decide to book Queens Hotel for dinner with John, as I can't think of anywhere more glamorous. Queens Hotel has always been the best hotel in the city centre – it was way beyond my price range for a meal or drinks when I was a student, so it will feel special going there now. I message John, telling him to meet me for pre-dinner cocktails in the hotel bar at seven pm. I get a message in return.

I spend ages getting ready, have a face pack, do my nails – the whole shebang. John is already sitting at the bar when I get there, and I'm surprised to see that he is wearing a suit. I have never seen him in a suit before. Which is what I say as I kiss him on the cheek as he stands up to greet me.

"And I have never seen you look more beautiful," is his unexpectedly suave reply. I find I am blushing.

"So why are you all suited and booted?" I ask.

"I had an interview earlier," he replies.

I laugh. "That makes two of us – I had one yesterday!"

John laughs, too. "Fancy us both coming up here for to try and get new jobs without telling each other. We try and get away for new lives, escape each other, and look what happens. So tell me about your interview. Where was it and how did it go?"

I tell John about my great success and ask about his interview. Which, by the sounds of things, did not go so well. His was at the BBC – it is quite a jump to move from a local newspaper newsroom to a TV one. He suspects that he will not be getting a job offer. He says: "So looks like I won't be joining you up here after all. Will you be alright making a move to another city all on your own?"

"I don't know if I will be."

"Why not, Grace? It sounds like a brilliant opportunity."

I look away. I can't tell John the truth. Not yet. Tonight I will act as though I do have a future. I turn back with a smile.

"You're absolutely right. It is a brilliant opportunity. I would be crazy not to accept it."

"And before you leave, looks like you will have a great story to tell about Iris the cat stealer."

This is something I do not want to talk about now, so I say: "Let's not talk about work, or anything to do with Dash-ford tonight."

"Cheers to that!" says John as he clinks his glass now half-full of martini with my glass nearly empty of Tequila Sunrise.

I don't know if the cocktails are particularly strong, or if I'm in a particularly light-hearted mood, but I find myself feeling giddy. As I study John's face, I realise I have never looked at him properly before. He might not be blessed with the matinee idol looks that Conrad had, but you know, I think he is actually far more attractive.

Maybe it is the way he looks at me and responds to me, he makes me feel that I'm both incredibly interesting and entertaining. With Conrad, I always felt that I was being patronised rather than admired, that I was lucky to get any attention from such a superior human. But with John I feel like I am a better person. A better person than I am.

For tonight, for just one night, I will allow myself to bathe in John's appreciation. And what the hell? I will show him tonight that I think he is rather special, too.

John picks up my mood of being happy and reckless and we race through our meal. When I invite him back to my hotel room for a coffee, John's face looks a picture. He obviously never expected such a brazen invitation from me. He soon rearranges his features so that he looks composed and says: "A coffee would be great."

Well. Coffee never happens, not until the morning anyhow.

Confession, Part Fifteen

Although I like to make out I'm the victim of circumstances, that my actions were not premeditated on my wedding day, actually I had very good reasons for getting rid of Conrad and Skye. On that day I despised them both. So much so that I wanted them dead.

I'm angry with myself for not facing up to the truth before my wedding, as that would have saved so much pain, not to mention a life. I think back to when I found the photographs under Conrad's wardrobe. There were other clues, too, that I deliberately ignored.

Ruth, from the first time she met him, hinted there was

something a bit "off" about Conrad. She never directly criti-
cised him, but would make comparisons between her relationship with Graham and mine with Conrad.

She would say how much she loved being with Graham
all the time, how they couldn't keep their hands off each
other, how sexy he made her feel. Usually, I would tell her
everything, no details too small about my life, but when she
began conversations like this, I would stay quiet. "Why are
you so secretive about Conrad?" she would ask. "Is it you
that has something to hide, or is it him?"

I would prevaricate by saying Conrad was a private
person.

"But you aren't private, Grace. You're an open book.
Too open. What are you frightened of revealing?"

What I didn't want to admit was that sex with Conrad
was not only infrequent but unrewarding.

Now, I can fully appreciate exactly how unrewarding
it was.

Chapter Seventeen

Saturday, 3 August 1996

John walks me to Leeds station after a hearty hotel breakfast, during which we keep smiling at each other stupidly. He plans to drive to his parents afterwards who live about an hour's drive away in Macclesfield. He had originally planned to drive there late last night, until I lured him to my hotel. He did call to tell them something had "come up", so that they wouldn't worry when he didn't turn up. John is considerate – I now know that for a fact. John offered to take me to meet his parents today, but I said that it was a bit soon.

On the train ride home, I start off in a brilliant mood, as my time with John has blanked out everything else. But half an hour into the journey, reality hits.

First thing I need to do is see Ruth when I get back. I message her and invite her over this evening.

"Only if you're going to come clean this time." she messages back.

I certainly am. I need to clear the air with Ruth before I go to the police.

At eight pm, I hear loud banging on the door, that could only come from someone with Ruth's power. The doorbell must have finally given up.

As soon as I open it, I instantly start to apologise.

"Oh come here, you!" Ruth says as she squeezes the life out of me in a big hug. Then we both start crying.

Ruth recovers her equilibrium before I do. "Right, Grace, that's enough of the soppy stuff. Let's get to it." She settles herself down on the settee.

"I am so sorry," I say again.

"No more apologising!" Ruth insists.

"It's just that I haven't made us any food. I have some crisps and wine, and that's it."

"Crisps and wine are fine for starters. If we're still hungry after your big reveal, we can order takeaway."

Soon, I'm sitting down beside her, holding tight to my large glass of red wine.

"I don't know where to begin. I have been keeping this hidden so tight within me for over two years. I don't know how to release it."

Ruth is matter of fact: "I will ask you questions then, and you answer them. Just one-word answers will do."

I nod.

"First question. When did you find out about Conrad? About his affair?"

"I think I had known about it for a while, but would never admit it to myself. It was on the wedding boat I found out for sure."

"When?"

"Not long after Mummy asked me to push her off. I went back outside, to regain my composure. I wanted a few minutes to myself. Also, I wanted to put back the chains that Mummy had undone. Before I got a chance to, Skye stumbled out." I pause. I feel myself staring to shake. "This is really hard to say," I mumble.

"You know what to do when you panic," says Ruth. "Breathe in for five, hold it for five, and breathe out for five. Come on, you can do this."

I start doing the breathing, with Ruth counting throughout to stop me hyperventilating.

Too soon, I think, Ruth orders me to continue the story.

"Skye came out. She said how she needed to tell me something. I said. 'You're pissed. Whatever it is, tell me when you're sober.'"

I pause again and repeat the slow-breathing exercise for a few breath cycles.

"Skye ignored me, and slurred: 'I have to tell you now, you stupid cow. Before you waste any more of your life with that bastard.'

"I was desperate not to hear what Skye wanted to tell me. I tried to ignore her. I turned my back on her to put back the chains, but Skye grabbed me and swung me around.

"I shouted: 'Leave me alone!' Skye lurched to the railings and gripped on tight with one hand – she needed their support to keep standing upright. She turned to me and that's when she said it: 'Your husband has been in love with someone else for years.'"

"I was calm, amazingly, when I replied: 'Oh, and I suppose that person is you? Go back inside, Skye, I'm fed up with hearing your pathetic stories.'

"Skye was beginning to edge along the railings towards the gap. I should have tried to move her away, but my mind was whirring. All I wanted was for her to stop talking. But she didn't. She went on: 'You know it isn't me. Everybody knows. They have hardly hidden it well. Conrad and Charlie have been lovers ever since they met at university.'

"I screamed: 'Shut up!' I felt such rage coursing through me. Still, she carried on: 'Those privileged tossers think they should have it all. Beautiful wives, flashy cars, fancy careers … and their dirty little secret.'

"'That's not true. That's not true,' I repeated, even though I knew it was. Skye's last words were: 'Why don't you ask Justin? He's slept with Charlie, too, a few times – he could give you some juicy details.'

"That is when I pushed her. She was standing exactly in the gap where the chains had been. It was easy. One second she was standing there; the next, she was gone."

There. I've said it. The world doesn't end. There is just silence. Ruth takes my hand in hers.

"I knew you blamed yourself. I just knew you thought it was you. I needed to hear you say it."

"Now, I need to tell the police."

Suddenly, Ruth is no longer so calm.

"Oh, don't be so ridiculous! You can't tell the police. What would be the point after all this time? What evidence is there?"

"I don't care, Ruth. I have to come clean. I can't carry on pretending."

Ruth drops my hand and stands up, rather menacingly, above me.

"We agreed, Grace."

"What did we agree?"

"We agreed at the time what happened. We went over and over it. How we followed Skye outside when we saw her go out as we were worried about her. How we tried to stop her going towards the gap, but we were too late—"

"Yes, but I just agreed to that story because I couldn't bear the consequences."

"But you never pushed her. I was there!"

"Then you know that she didn't just fall ..."

Ruth sits back down on the settee again. Staring intently into my eyes, she says: "This is like the towel rail in the bathroom all over again."

"What?" I'm flummoxed.

"You remember. You have a habit of making stuff up and convincing yourself it's true. A habit of taking the blame and feeling guilty for everything. Your mother trained you to do that. Which is why you took the blame for breaking the handrail in my parents' bathroom."

The incident comes back to me. "I thought I did break it."

"No, you didn't. It was me. We were mucking about in the bathroom and I started using the handrail as a pretend ballet barre and pulled it off the wall by accident. When my mum stormed in to find out what was going on, you immediately said you had been swinging on it. We ended up having a fight about it and my mum got totally confused."

"I am confused now. The details aren't clear in my head, but I remember thinking it was my fault."

"That's the point I am making. Whenever something bad happens, you always take the blame."

I sigh. "This isn't just 'something bad' that happened. I can remember my wedding day so clearly. I go over it in my head every night. I know it was my fault that Skye died. You can't stop me. I'm going to the police tomorrow."

Ruth sighs. After a pause, she says: "I can't let you take the blame this time. It was me who pushed Skye, not you."

Confession, Part Sixteen

It was a messy evening. First I confess; then Ruth confesses. I must say, Ruth was so adamant that it was her, I almost believe her. I can now see her story in my head as clearly as my own.

Her version of events is that she saw me going out on the deck with Skye, so came out soon after to check everything was okay. It was not okay. Skye and I were in a messy embrace, Skye holding onto me for (literally) dear life, talking madly into my ear, whilst I was trying to push her away, saying: "No, it isn't true! It isn't true!"

Ruth came up to us and tried to separate us. She didn't mean to push us apart so violently. So violently that I fell to the floor of the deck whilst Skye plunged to the gap in the railings. And then over the edge.

Ruth has never known her own strength.

What we do agree on is what happened immediately after Skye fell.

I remember at this point that we were together, but whether Ruth came out just after I pushed Skye or was there in the actual moment, I'm not so clear about.

Instantly, Ruth took charge. She led me inside the boat

and sat me down before she marched off to tell the captain that a guest had just fallen off the back deck.

That was when the party ended. There were announcements; there were sirens. The police came on board. It all seemed to happen in both slow motion and very quickly at the same time.

Despite the speed, the river lifeboat could not find Skye. Her body was not recovered until a few days later.

The rest of that evening was all tears and loss.

I was not just crying for Skye; I was crying for the death of my marriage. When Conrad tried to comfort me on the boat, I pushed him away. Justin came over to talk to me, but I put my hand up: "Not now, Justin."

Justin looked coldly at me. "I saw her fall. We need to talk about it."

"Yes, but not now, Justin."

It was a sorry sight, all of us leaving the boat at Kingston. There were more police waiting for us on the wharf, and we were all told to get in touch with them if we wished to make statements about anything we had seen.

We all slowly got on the coach that we had booked to take the guests back to Richmond, where they had left their cars or were staying in hotels. We were a subdued, sorry lot. No one was as sorry as me. Conrad and I sat at the front. As people walked past, a few stopped to offer their condolences. As Mummy went past, she muttered: "I knew that woman would ruin your big day."

Conrad and I sat looking straight ahead. He reached for my hand, and I snatched it away.

We got off the bus outside the Register Office and said muted farewells. Ruth gave me a hug and whispered: "It will all be okay, we will get through this." Conrad and I walked with Ruth and Graham to their car. Graham dropped us both off at Conrad's flat.

When we got inside, I sank down onto his dark, grey velvet sofa. He had such good taste. Conrad sat down next to me.

"Get away from me," I said quietly.

Conrad looked surprised.

"I know this is difficult for you, but we have to stick together through this. You have to let me support you." He tried to put his arm around me. I jumped up. I had never hated anyone so much in my life. It should have been him I pushed off the boat. Everything was his fault – this whole mess, all his fault.

"I know the truth about you Conrad," I said.

"Sorry. What?"

In a monotone, I said: "I know about you and Charlie."

Conrad stood up and tried to hug me again. Again, I pushed him away.

"Whoever told you, and I imagine it was Skye, that there is anything more to my friendship with Charlie is wrong. There have always been rumours; people have always been jealous of us, but we're just good friends. Bloody good friends."

"Bloody good friends? Well, you're a bloody good liar!" I screamed. "Don't bother making up stories anymore. I know. I have known for ages. I just didn't want to face the truth."

Conrad sat down on the sofa again, his dark grey suit complementing it perfectly. He looked like he was advertising the furniture, adorning it. Even now, at the moment of our destruction, he looked immaculate.

Tearfully he said: "Please don't leave me, Grace. I need you."

"You need me to complete your perfect life. You want it all."

"I will never see Charlie again; I will give him up for you. I love you. Don't leave me."

Considering what a state I was in, it was remarkable how eloquent I remained. "You should stop seeing Charlie, but not to keep me. That's no longer an option. You should give Charlie up because he is using you, like you used me. He will never give up his family for you. You don't deserve my advice, but here it is. Stop pretending. Stop leading a double life. Find a man you can be happy with, honest with and open with. Whatever you do, don't do to another woman what you have done to me."

I didn't want to stay with Conrad that night, but at first I couldn't think where to go. I didn't want to go back to Mummy's and face her; I didn't want to go back to my flat and be surrounded by all of Skye's possessions. I packed a bag and called a taxi. I went to Ruth's.

Poor Ruth. We were both in a state that night, and I have never allowed her to leave my, or rather our, personal nightmare. We spent weeks going over the events again and again, but I never quite believed the story we stuck to – that it was not our fault that Skye went over the edge. That we were just onlookers.

Over the months, the years, that followed, I reconstructed the evening so that it made sense to me. I can see so clearly that I pushed Skye. I can now, thanks to Ruth, also see her version of events.

How can I find out which one is true? Then it hits me. There is someone who saw it all. Someone who threatened to go to the police to tell them everything. Last time I saw Justin was at Skye's funeral.

Funerals are not known for being a fun time, but out of

all the funerals I have been to, Skye's was the worst. As Skye had once been a minor celebrity, there was a flurry of interest in the media following her death. Skye would have been disappointed, had she still been around, just how quickly she was forgotten, though. How few newspaper inches were devoted to her short life. There were no plaudits from Mick Jagger, Sting, Bob Geldof, or any of the other famous men she said she had been "close to".

She would also have been furious to find out that no one suspected foul play. Most items about her death focused on her public slide into alcoholism and drug addiction.

Despite the media coverage, the funeral was small. Even Skye's mother did not turn up. Justin had gone to great lengths to track her down in America. He had had to write to her, as she couldn't be contacted by phone or email. She replied with a short note saying that she would not be able to attend the service. No explanation, no words about Skye. No wonder Skye was so damaged.

Justin was in a state. Not surprising, since he had been the person who had organised the funeral, the person who had identified Skye's body. The only person, he later said, who really cared.

It was a bright, warm July day. A Wednesday, just over two weeks after the wedding, in a church in Dashford. Conrad had spoken to me on the phone, asked me if I wanted him to attend, but I told him to stay away. Ruth came to support me. Ruth, Justin, and I were the only people representing her friends. A few people from Now!Network were there, and a handful from the newspaper she had been working for when she died. This tiny group was dwarfed by the dimensions of the church, highlighting how unloved Skye was.

Justin hardly spoke to me. When I tried to catch his eye,

he looked away. After the service, I went up to Justin outside the church. He wouldn't let me hug him; he glared at me and said: "You're lucky I didn't go to the police. I'm still thinking about telling them what really happened, so I wouldn't get too comfortable if I were you." Then he turned and walked away.

I must call Justin. It is too late to try now. Ruth and I spent so long talking, crying, and talking that she didn't leave until the early hours.

Chapter Eighteen

LOCAL HOUSE PRICES GO THROUGH THE ROOF

By Grace O'Neill

The last 12 months have seen a dramatic rise in the average cost of a three-bedroomed house in the Dashford area. A local estate

Sunday, 4 August 1996

I wake up, startled. Startled that I have even been asleep after last night. Realising there are no cats bothering me for food, I jump up and rush downstairs. Phew! There they are, curled up together on the sofa. It must be earlier than I imagine if they aren't hungry yet.

The clock on the oven says it is six am. Hours to fill before I can contact Justin.

I make a list. A list of all the things I need to do to the

house, including replace the doorbell battery. One way or another, I will be going away and will need to make sure this place is in a fine enough state to rent out.

Then I go for a run, have a shower, and try to eat. I make toast, but can't swallow it.

Is nine am on a Sunday too early to call Justin, I wonder? I decide it isn't.

He picks up on the second ring.

I mumble, "Hello Justin", and he cuts me off quickly.

"Grace."

"Is this too early?" I ask.

"No, it is far too late. I have been meaning to get in touch for ages. I'm so sorry, Grace."

"Why are you sorry?"

"Well, the last words I said to you were awful. Blaming you for Skye's death. Implying you had murdered her. We must meet up. I need to see you, apologise properly. When are you free?"

"Now?" I say. "I could catch a train into London, be there in an hour or so?"

Justin agrees to meet me for cocktails at a bar in Soho that used to be a favourite of Skye's. I had suggested lunch might be better, but Justin insisted it had to be cocktails. That we needed to toast Skye in an appropriate way.

It isn't long before I am perched on a bar stool, surrounded by mirrors and chandeliers, sipping another Tequila Sunrise. I have arrived earlier than we agreed, but I only have to wait five minutes before Justin arrives.

He looks great. A different person from the dishevelled, devastated man I last saw two years ago. He comes in for a hug straight away.

"We really should have done this sooner," he says. "I have missed you."

"I have missed you, too, but thought you never wanted to see me again."

"I didn't at first. But let's move to a quiet table and talk properly, before I get all emotional and embarrassing."

We take our drinks to a corner of the room.

"Let me take a look at you," says Justin. "Hmm. Not too bad" is his verdict. "Maybe cut a few inches off your hair? It looks good, but you can have too much of a good thing, you know ..."

"Well you look fabulous," I reply.

"Thank you, darling. It took me a while to get my act together. I was almost as bad a drinker as Skye was. You would think her death would have been a lesson to me. But it was a lesson that took a while to sink in. I know I'm having a cocktail now, but this is, believe it or not, unusual for me these days. Anyway, let's make a toast. To Skye!"

"To Skye!" I say, clinking glasses.

There is a bit of an awkward pause. I suppose neither of us wants to start the heavy conversation that we know is inevitable. I decide I have to know, right now.

"Justin, you said it was lucky for me you didn't go to the police? Why?"

"You should know why – you were there. I could have made a statement, but after thinking about it, I thought there was no point. No point in ruining any more lives. I realised it was an accident. An accident waiting to happen."

"Obviously I was there, Justin, but Ruth says my memory is playing tricks on me, and that I'm remembering it wrong."

"Well, she would say that, wouldn't she."

This is getting me no closer to finding out what Justin saw. So I ask him directly.

Only to get yet another version of events.

Justin says that he came to the back deck for some fresh air, only to discover there was a fight going on. Ruth, Skye, and I were all screaming at each other. Then things became physical.

He saw Skye falling backwards. He expected her to be stopped by the safety chains, but no, she fell clean off the boat. There were no chains!

"So, Grace, who removed the safety chains? Was it you? Because whoever took them away is the person who killed Skye."

I explain that it was my mother who had removed them, and that I had never got the chance to put them back.

Justin laughed. "I know it is completely inappropriate to laugh, but it is just so funny that it was your mother who was responsible for Skye's death. She must be burning in hell now. Which really wasn't her plan. To be honest, Skye was no angel either, so they are probably down there together ..."

I have to know exactly who pushed Skye. I suppose in a way it doesn't matter – neither Ruth nor I pushed her deliberately – but I just need to know. Because if it was me, I still feel I should go to the police.

This is what I explain to Justin.

"Oh no, darling. You mustn't go the police. It definitely wasn't you. And it wasn't really Ruth either."

"What do you mean?"

"Well, I can't swear absolutely, as it was a long time ago. But I do distinctly remember seeing Skye going for you, and Ruth blocking her. It was the force of hitting Ruth that sent her tumbling backwards. Must have been like rebounding off a brick wall – no offence to your friend, but she is rather well built. I certainly never saw you push her. I suppose there is the chance that Ruth might have met Skye's onslaught with more force than she needed to ... But there was no deliberate push. It was an accident. A terrible accident."

I sigh, a deep, deep sigh. "Such a waste of a life."

Justin agrees. "Skye had everything going for her – talent, beauty, intelligence ... But it wasn't enough. Waste is the word... Let's face it, she was wasted nearly all the time at the end. It would be nice to imagine that if she hadn't died, she could have got her act together one day, but I'm not so sure. She seemed hell bent on sticking to her path of self-destruction.

"Immediately after her death I tortured myself with thoughts of how bad a friend I had been, that somehow I could have saved her. I also blamed you. I'm sorry, but I did. She absolutely loved you, but I was convinced just after her death that you had failed her.

"Over time, I realised it wasn't either of our faults. Ultimately, Skye was the cause of her own demise. If she hadn't fallen off your boat, some other tragedy would have befallen her. Or one of her suicide attempts would have succeeded. As you said, it was such a waste of a life."

I am crying. Proper tears over the loss of someone with so much potential. Not tears of self-pity, which are what I have been shedding so copiously over the years. I realise I have never properly mourned Skye, because I was so wrapped up in self-blame and sadness about the end of my relationship with Conrad.

Justin moves closer to comfort me. "We should do something to commemorate Skye. For the bright light she could have been."

Wiping my eyes on a silk handkerchief that Justin offers me, I agree. "Yes, you're absolutely right. What do you think would be appropriate?"

"This isn't a bad start," says Justin, "having cocktails in one of her favourite bars."

"What else did she love doing?" I ask.

"Her main hobby was sleeping with married men, but I have already done my fair share of that. Those days, I'm pleased to say, are over. Skye always loved to dance ..."

Justin and I agree that we must have a big night out. Wear our most sparkly clothes and go clubbing into the early hours. I used to love dancing, too, but it has been so long since I have. We set a date for the next weekend.

We have a lot of other catching up to do. I can hear myself saying that I'm about to start a new life in Leeds, and that I have met a man I care about. I can't believe what I'm saying – that I'm now actually going to move on with my life, rather than just hand myself into a police station. There is nothing to stop me moving forwards now, is there?

Justin tells me how he has worked his way up his advertising agency and is creative director. He also has a long-term partner, whom he lives with. A barrister called Jacob. He asks me if I have stayed in contact with Conrad. I shake my head and explain how we hadn't remained on civil terms, or rather, that I hadn't.

Justin shakes his head. "You know, you mustn't blame Conrad too much. He doesn't have parents like mine who can accept who their son is. I ran into him a few weeks ago in a bar. He was looking as devastatingly handsome as always."

"Is he still seeing Charlie?" I can't resist asking.

"No. He told me he is single but mingling. In search of the perfect man. You can imagine, it is hard to find someone who meets his high standards. I always thought he was far too good for Charlie."

Justin realises I might be offended by what he has just

said, so quickly adds: "He was not too good for you, of course! It was absolutely the other way around! Skye was always saying how you deserved better."

It is inevitable that the conversation keeps drifting back to Skye. She is the reason we are together now, the reason we became friends in the first place. The reason we are going to party next week.

We will always be sad about Skye, but now it is time to start feeling some joy, too. Her life should be celebrated as well as mourned.

Chapter Nineteen

Saturday, 20 March 1997

I am woken up by a mug of coffee being thrust at me. "No lie in today, Grace! We have a lot to do!"

I sit up slowly and take the mug. Yes, we do have a lot on today. There is our usual Saturday run and swim, followed by a marathon of cleaning and food shopping. We need to prepare for our special visitors. Luckily, there isn't room for them all to stay overnight in our small house; I'm not sure I could face Horrible Horace and Fighty Fergus for a night as well as an afternoon and evening. Yes, today Ruth and her family are coming to visit us. I'm so excited, as it has been months since I have seen any of them.

I sit upright. "Where are the cats?" It still feels wrong to be woken up by a human, rather than a cat.

John replies: "Miro is asleep in his favourite sunny spot. Not sure about Blake. Probably out trying to deplete the local wildlife population."

We are living just outside Huddersfield, in a rented stone cottage with a large garden that keeps me busy now that I'm a keen gardener, and provides the cats with a large hunting ground. They have three loud bells each on their collars, so the toll on the local small wild animals has been relatively modest. Just two frogs so far.

By the time Ruth and her family arrive, everything is spick and span. John only moved in a month ago, after much debate as to whether it was too soon, and I occasionally have moments when I think maybe it was. As much as I love him, it is difficult getting used to someone else's funny ways. He leaves his clothes everywhere; I regularly find socks on the dining room table and pants on the stairs (on the way to the washing machine, apparently). I can't get rid of him now, as the cats absolutely adore him.

It doesn't help that I had this house to myself first for so long and could live exactly as I pleased. John used to come for weekends before he landed a job as the editor of the *Manchester Evening Post*. At first, John said he would find his own place, but eventually we decided we might as well give it a go living together. It will make or break us, we decided. And just as long as his underwear manages to make its way to the washing machine in one trip in the future, without stops on random pieces of furniture, my bet is that it will make us.

Ruth walks down our front path holding a large cake tin. "No hugs until I have put this down. I have been cradling it carefully since we left home four hours ago. I'm desperate to get rid of it!"

"What have you baked?" I ask.

"Not me – it's from that old witch Iris. She has made you a chocolate cake, as she said it was your favourite."

Ruth might call Iris a witch, but since I left Dashford, she has been a great friend to the old woman. She must have needed someone else to look after once I left town. Iris has been through the wars; getting questioned by the police scared her. She also went to a local lawyer to confess to pushing over that poor man on the bike. None of her crimes led to an arrest; she was just cautioned and given a warning about cat stealing. As far as the bike "accident" was concerned, Iris's lawyer said her memory of events could not be relied upon and there was not enough of a case to arrest her for accidental murder – he explained there had been no reckless behaviour on her part.

I spent many days after this helping Iris in her garden and listening to her worries, but in actuality, those days were spent helping me. Iris's experience clarified it in my head that, even if my memory of pushing Skye was correct, which I now doubted, I was no murderer.

No more cats have gone mysteriously missing in Dashford as far as we know since Iris tried to catnap the mayor's cat. Ruth claimed one of the reasons she spent so much time visiting Iris was to check that no one else's pets were being kept hostage there, but I think Ruth has become rather fond of Iris now, just like I did. I miss Iris.

I also miss Skye. Since I have stopped torturing myself with guilt, I no longer dwell on the bad times. Going out with Justin dancing helped to bring back the more joyful memories. I have been commemorating Skye in Leeds by leaving flowers at all of her old student haunts. I even took a large bunch of chrysanthemums to the dentist's surgery Skye took me to all those years ago. The receptionist seemed surprised, but also touched that I had brought flowers to brighten up the waiting room. Mr Roister, whom Skye may or may not have had an affair with, is now my dentist. He is a great dentist. I'm pleased to report my teeth have been giving me no trouble whatsoever since I moved here.

From being a relatively peaceful haven of calm before Ruth and her lot arrived, our cottage is now full of shouting and laughter. As they all pour inside, my tightest embrace is saved for Horace – he is still my favourite.

After coffee, orange squash, and chocolate cake, the boys and men go outside to play football. "How traditional!" I say as Ruth and I load up the dishwasher. "Men outside having fun; women exhausting themselves in the kitchen."

"How dreadful. We used to be such good feminists. We will have to make sure to put the situation right later on by going out and having a few pints whilst our other halves prepare the dinner and look after the kids."

It makes me feel a bit peculiar hearing John described as my other half. Peculiar in a good way.

"Cheers!" I say four hours later as Ruth and I sit in the pub as planned. "Not such a bad life!"

Not such a bad life at all.

Epilogue

2pm, Monday, 29 March 1997

Sitting at her desk at *The Yorkshire Mail*, Grace is startled by her phone ringing, waking her from her post-lunch stupor. She answers on the second ring.

"Hello, *Yorkshire Mail*. Grace speaking."

"Hi Grace, it is Charlotte here, from your old office."

Grace pauses before answering. "Oh hello, Charlotte, so lovely to hear from you, I hope you have some shocking office scandal you want to share with me..."

"Well, actually I have! I was scandalised to receive a huge bunch of flowers this morning. Then even more surprised to find they were from you, with a note that reads 'Thank you.'. I just wanted to say thanks. And ask why you sent them?"

"Because you saved my life, in a way..."

"By helping you out by writing the odd feature?"

"No, because when I was struggling, and confused about everything, I used to call the Samaritans. It was the only thing that helped. I don't know if I ever spoke to you, but as you are the only Samaritan I know, now that I'm feeling so much better, I wanted to make a gesture of gratitude. And please pass on my thanks to all the other volunteers."

"It is so nice to be appreciated," Charlotte says. "Before you go, I want to say what a pleasure it was working with you. You were always a kind, generous colleague, which is rare in a newspaper. So *Dashford Times*'s loss is definitely *Yorkshire Mail*'s gain.

"Also, should you ever need to call the Samaritans again, never feel afraid of sharing all your feelings. You will never be judged, and everything you say will be always kept in the strictest confidence."

What Charlotte wanted to add, but was too professional to do so, was that it would also be taken with a pinch of salt. Charlotte remembered clearly all of the calls she had taken from Grace, and she had realised from the moment she met Grace in person that she couldn't possibly be a murderer. Charlotte had done some research and read the old news cuttings about the tragic death of Skye, and could imagine only too well how something like that happening at your wedding would mess with your mind.

Charlotte was pleased that Grace was now thinking straight. Although she almost missed those calls in the middle of the night from someone claiming to be a killer. They added some intrigue and distraction to what was often a very grim night.

Coming soon
The new domestic thriller from Daney Parker

DEADY

Does it take a psychopath to kill a psychopath?

It is October 2020 when Sarah and her husband Henry, find Sarah's father dead in his own bathroom. This is no surprise to them – on the contrary, it is a relief. Because their plan to murder him looks like it has succeeded.

As for many other people in the UK, 2020 with all its lockdowns and national tragedies has been a tough year for Sarah, her husband and their student children. Relationships become strained, but even so, what leads two such "normal" people to want to commit murder? It is clear that Sarah's father Brian is a psychopath, but it also seems that there may be other psychopaths in the family. Hidden secrets come to the surface that explain the ghastly reasons for wanting to commit a ghastly crime. No one is quite who they seem to be at first in this twisty-turny novel that explores relationships from all angles, in particular, the darker parts that are usually kept well hidden.

Acknowledgments

Thank you to Katherine Price for helping me in so many ways, so much wisdom and such a brilliant writer, she puts me to shame. I am sorry to all my friends I have forced the first draft of this book upon, but thank you Nicola Lowit, Michele Teboul, Paul Gowers and Vanessa Collu for reading it. Plus thank you to the brilliant publisher of Creative Moment magazine for her encouragement, Lucy Smith. I am really grateful to my wonderful editor Claire Strombeck for her enthusiasm and hard work. Shout out to Diane Messidoro for nagging me to write and her brilliant way with commas. Thank you also to Martin Small for my author pic.

Last thanks to my family for also reading this, Lyra, Ellis and my mother. Thank you especially to Julian, for always being there even when I am far away.

About the Author

Daney Parker has loved working with words for as long as she can remember. She is delighted that she has managed to make a living following her passion – copywriting, publishing in magazines and now writing domestic thrillers. As well as writing, Daney likes to chat... she is particularly good at asking probing questions, getting people to confess their deepest, darkest secrets. So if you ever meet up with her, be careful what you reveal.

Daney writes in the Isle of Wight, has two children, one husband and two cats.

You can link up with the author on her website:

www.daneyparker.co.uk

Printed in Great Britain
by Amazon

27107227R00119